Paul Howard is Chief Sportswriter with *The Sunday Tribune* in Dublin. He was Sports Journalist of the Year in 1998.

His previous books include *Celtic Warrior* (1995), *The Joy* (1996) and *The Miseducation of Ross O'Carroll-Kelly* (2000).

# Roysh Here Roysh Now

*Ross O'Carroll-Kelly –
the teenage dirtbag years*

# Paul Howard

The Sunday Tribune

First published by *The Sunday Tribune*,
15 Lower Baggot Street, Dublin 2, Ireland.
Set in 11 point on 14 Stone serif

## ISBN 0-9526035-5-1

© **Paul Howard, 2001**

## ross@tribune.ie

**Designed, edited & produced by: Gerard Siggins**

**Illustrations: Dave Gorman**
**Back cover photograph: Declan Shanahan**

*For Karen*

# ACKNOWLEDGEMENTS

Thank you, Karen for your love, your sense of humour
and the inside information that gives Ross his soul.
Sorry for not being Johnny Wilkinson.
Thank you mum and dad for thirty great years.
Thank you Vincent and Richard, you funny bastards.
Thank you Ger Siggins for editing the book and
being a great source of, well, everything.
Thank you Matt Cooper for your forebearance and support.
Thank you Jim Farrelly and Mark Jones for the same.
Thank you Deirdre Sheerin, oh Rose of Delgany,
for proof-reading the book.
And thank you Maureen Gillespie and the army
who've contributed in one way and the other.

# Chapter One

*The one where Ross gets arrested*

WOMEN have peripheral vision, Emer goes, which is why they always know when a goy is, like, checking them out, roysh, and why goys never know when they're actually being checked out themselves. She can't remember where she read this, it might have been in *Red* or *Marie Claire* or some other shit. I'm not really listening. I'm waiting for my food to arrive and throwing the odd sly look at Sorcha, my ex who's, like, doing the DBS in Carysfort, and who's looking totally amazing, just back from Montauk, the pink Ralph Lauren shirt I bought her for her birthday showing off her tan and shit. Aoife asks her if she thinks Starbucks will ever open a place in, like, Dublin, roysh, and Sorcha says OH MY GOD she hopes they do because she SO misses their orange mocha chip frappuccinos and Aoife says she misses their caramel macchiatos and they both carry on naming different types of coffee, roysh, both in American accents, which is weird because they were only in the States for, like, the summer.

The food takes ages to arrive, roysh, and when the spa of a waitress we've been given finally brings it she forgets the focking cutlery and Fionn turns around to her and goes, "I suppose a fork is out of the question?" The waitress, roysh, we're talking a TOTAL focking howiya here, she's like, "What did you say?" and I'm there, "Are we supposed to eat this with our FOCKING hands?" and she stands there for a few seconds and tries to give me a filthy, roysh, but then she just, like, scuttles off to the kitchen and Fionn high-fives me, and Christian high-fives Oisínn, and Emer and Aoife shake their heads, and Zoey, who's like second year commerce with German in UCD, SO like Mena Suvari it's unbelievable, she throws her eyes up to heaven and goes, "Children".

Emer takes a sip of her Ballygowan, roysh, and she goes, "Oh my God, you should have SEEN the state of the toilets in college yesterday", and all of a sudden I'm there, "Where's college?" totally flirting my orse off with her, even though I've no real interest – it's just, like, Sorcha's sitting there going totally ballistic? – and Emer goes, "I'm in LSB. Marketing, advertising and public relations". I'm like, "Cool", but then Fionn, roysh, he totally blows my chances by launching into this new theory he has about why public toilets are always so, like, gross. He's there, "You have to be pretty desperate for a shit to use a public toilet in the first place. And let's face it, a desperate shit is never a pretty shit." And Zoey, roysh, she holds up her bottle of Panna and goes, "HELLO? Some of us are trying to EAT here."

Erika arrives then, roysh – total babe, the spit of Denise Richards – and she throws her shopping bags onto the chair beside me and goes, "Oh my God, is it my imagination or have the shops in town started hiring the biggest knackers in Ireland as security guards?" Emer says something about the Celtic Tiger, roysh, about them, like, not being able to get staff because of it, and Erika goes, "I'm sorry, I will NOT be looked up and down by men with focking buckles on their shoes", and then she orders a Diet Coke and storts texting Jenny to find out what she's doing for Hallowe'en weekend.

Sorcha takes off her scrunchy, slips it onto her wrist, shakes her hair free and then smoothes it back into a low ponytail again, puts it back in the scrunchy and then pulls five or six, like, strands of hair loose again. She knows I'm staring at her because her face is red, roysh, and I'm pretty sure she still has feelings for me. I ask her how college is going and she goes, "It's amazing. Fiona and Grace are on the same course". I'm like, "Cool. Are you still thinking of going into Human Resources?" and she goes, "I don't know. Me and Fiona are thinking of maybe going to Australia for a year. When we're finished, like."

She's checking me out for a reaction, roysh, but I don't say anything and she goes, "I heard you got into UCD". I'm there, "Oh yeah, mum said she met you". And she goes, "A sports scholarship, Ross. Congrats." I can't make out whether she's being, like, bitch and shit? I'm just like, "Yeah, it's the sports management course. I don't start for another couple of weeks." And she goes, "That's supposed to be a really good course. It's only, like, one day of lectures a week or something." I pick up my tuna melt and I'm like, "I don't care what the course is like. I'm just looking forward to getting back playing good rugby again."

Erika finishes texting Jenny, roysh, takes a sip out of her Coke and, like, makes a face. She pushes it over to me and goes, "Taste that, Ross. That's not Diet Coke, is it?" I take a sip, roysh, but she doesn't wait for my opinion, just grabs the waitress and goes, "Excuse me, I asked for a Diet Coke." The waitress is like, "That is Diet Coke". And Erika goes, "HELLO? I think I KNOW what Diet Coke tastes like." Your one picks it up and says she'll, like, change it, but Erika grabs her by the arm, looks her up and down and goes, "If I was earning two pounds an hour, I'd probably have an attitude problem as well."

Zoey's talking about some goy called Jamie from second year Orts who is SO like Richard Fish it's unbelievable, and Sorcha and Emer stort having this, like, debate about whether Richard Fish is actually sexy or whether it's just because he's a bastard to women, when all of a sudden, roysh, the manager comes over and tells us he wants us to leave. We're all there, "You needn't think we're paying", and as we're going out the door the waitress goes, "Snobs", under her breath, roysh, and Erika gives her this total filthy and goes, "Being working class is nothing to be proud of, you know".

JP puts his name down for *Who Wants To Be A Millionaire?*, roysh, pretty much for the laugh, because he's not, like, intelligent or anything, not like Fionn, but OH MY GOD he focking goes and gets picked, roysh, and he's there, "Goys, you have SO got to help me out here". So all of the goys, roysh, we're talking me, Christian, Fionn, Oisínn, we get tickets to, like, sit in the studio audience and of course me and Fionn, roysh, we end up going to the M1 for a few scoops beforehand, the two boys arrive out at RTE totally shit-faced and we're talking the middle of the afternoon here? We manage to find our seats, roysh, miracle of focking miracles, and we're sitting there just, like, trying to hold in the laughter basically, and all of a sudden who arrives only this bird Frederika, JP's new squeeze who's, like, first year Russian and Byzantine studies in UCD and who is going to get the serious flick if JP manages to win any money today, even though she doesn't know it. She's actually alright looking, roysh, a little bit like Charlize Theron except with no chest and we are talking totally here. The second she sits down, Fionn leans over to me, roysh, and he goes, "Anyone with any information on the whereabouts of Frederika's baps, would they please contact gardaí at Donnybrook."

I break my shite laughing, roysh, but Frederika obviously hasn't heard it because she sits down and asks how we are, roysh, and before we have a chance to answer she tells us that she's ACTUALLY been shopping all morning for clothes which is why she is SO depressed and then she storts bitching about Cliona, her best friend, who she had a huge row with in Pia Bang and who she says is SUCH a sly bitch it's unbelievable. Cliona, if I'm thinking about the right girl, roysh, is not only a sly bitch, but an ugly one as well, even though she has a totally amazing bod. She's what we call a bobfoc, which is, like Body Off *Baywatch*, Face Off *Crimewatch*? Frederika, roysh, she says she told Cliona she was SO not moving up to a 26 which is basically what Cliona wanted all along and even though Cliona said she wasn't suggesting it just to be a bitch she actually was, she SO was, and in the end apparently Cliona just focked off and left her and when they saw each other later on in Danos they just totally ignored each other, which is basically what me and Fionn are doing to Frederika at this stage.

I'm actually very, very pissed, roysh, and I notice for the first time that Christian and the rest of the goys have also arrived and they're, like, sitting on the other side of Frederika, and when Christian sees me he goes, "May the Force Be With You", and I actually return the greeting, can you believe that? So we're all sitting there anyway, totally bored out of our faces, watching all the focking contestants and waiting for JP's turn, and about an hour into it, he's up, roysh, and he comes on wearing his Castlerock jersey and we're all there going, "Whooooaahhh!" and Gay Byrne's like, "You seem to have a few fans in here today", and we're all there giving it, "Castlerock Uber Alles", giving it loads, roysh, and Gay Byrne's like, "Okay. Okay. Lovely. Okay. Alright", the way he does.

So he does the introduction, roysh, and it's like, name JP Conroy, age 20, occupation working for the old man, or whatever he said, director of Conroy-Barry Estate Agents and Auctioneers, even though he's, like, fock-all qualifications, which we give him total stick over. So anyway, roysh, the first question is, like, SO easy. It's like, "Who went up the hill with Jack?" We're all there, 'Duh'. He goes, "Jill" and Gay Byrne's like, "Well done, well done". A hundred bills straight off. The next question is, like, "How many colours are there in a rainbow?" and we're all like, "Oh my God, he's doing to make a total spa of himself here," but he goes, "Seven", roysh, and Gay Byrne goes, "You've got two hundred pounds" and we're all there, "How the fock did he know that?"

So anyway, roysh, JP's there getting totally carried away with himself now, SO cocky it's unbelievable. He's, like, slouching back, one arm hanging over the back of the chair, his legs sprawled out in front of him and he's, like, flying through the questions, so the thousand pound one arrives, roysh, and it's, "When was the Easter Rising?" and the answers are, like, "1915, 1916, 1917 or 1918". We all just look at each other in the audience and Frederika goes, "Oh my God that is SUCH an unfair question", and it's, like, obvious from where we're sitting that JP doesn't have a focking breeze either? His arm isn't slung over the back of the chair anymore. He's got his head, like, in his hands, roysh, and he's going, "I know this. I so know this". Gay Byrne's there, "Did you do history at school?" and JP's like, "Yeah, but I was on the S". And Gay Byrne's like, "Okay. Lovely. Alright".

Eventually, roysh, Gay reminds him that he still has, like, his lifelines left and JP goes, "Alroysh, I'm going to have to phone a friend" but we're all there going, "Who the fock is going to know the answer to that?" So they make the call, roysh, and the next thing I hear is this mobile going off beside me and the ring is, like, the Eminem song, 'Stan'? It's coming from Fionn's pocket. The whole audience is staring at Fionn, roysh, and we're talking totally here, as he roots through his pocket looking for the thing and, even though Fionn is a total Einstein and could normally answer a question like that in his sleep, he is so totally shit-faced that I'm actually scared of what he's going to say.

When he eventually finds his phone, roysh, after like two minutes of fumbling around, he answers it and, like, sits up really straight in his seat, trying his best to, like, sober up, but he's focked and he goes, "Yello?" And the whole audience bursts out laughing. We can hear his voice, like, echoing around the studio, roysh, really bad feedback and shit, and Gay Byrne's there, "Hello, Fionn. This is Gay Byrne from *Who Wants To Be A Millionaire?*" We're all like, 'No shit, Sherlock'. Fionn's looking around him, like he doesn't know where the fock he is.

Then JP goes, "Fionn, I need your help here and we're talking big-style. There's a thousand notes riding on this question, roysh. So it's, like, when was the Easter Rising?" Fionn goes, "I don't know, I was on the..." and JP's like, "No, just listen. Was it 1915, 1916, 1917 or 1918?" Fionn closes his eyes, roysh, and bows his head and it actually looks like he's conked out, but just as I'm about to nudge him to, like, wake him up, roysh, he looks up and goes, "Nineteen-fifteen, is that, like, a quarter past seven, is it?"

Oh my God we all burst our shites laughing, roysh, and the next thing we hear is this goy, the floor manager or something shouting "CUT", and someone else going, "Get those idiots out of here", and the next thing we know, roysh, these focking bouncers appear from nowhere and stort, like dragging us out. We're talking JP and everything. It was like something off Jerry Springer.

Of course JP is going totally ballistic and he's, like, shouting back into the studio, "I still have two lifelines left, you assholes", and Frederika tells him that he didn't actually lose, that Fionn got us thrown out, roysh, and JP storts giving him filthies, so me and Christian decide to get Fionn the fock out of there before JP rams the goy's glasses down his throat. We tell JP we're bringing him back to the M1, roysh, and he says he's glad because he needs a drink, and as we're leaving, roysh, I can hear Frederika telling one of the bouncers that he better hope for his sake that her jacket isn't ripped because it's actually a Karen Millen original and when he says he doesn't give a shit she tells him he has an attitude problem.

It's, like, two o'clock on Sunday afternoon, roysh, and the traffic on the Stillorgan dual carriageway is unbelievable. We're talking bomper to bomper here. I mean, what is the focking point of having a car that can do seventy if focking forty is the fastest you're able to go? Mind you, roysh, you get up above seventy in this thing, the old dear's focking Micra, and bits stort to fall off. Not that there's much danger of that happening with this bitch in front of me. She is SO trying to fock me over, roysh, driving really slowly and then, like, speeding up when she sees the traffic lights on orange, trying to make me miss the lights, trying to fock me over. I turn on the radio and flick through the presets but there's, like, fock-all on. Samantha Mumba is actually on three different stations at the same time and I'm wondering if this is, like, a world record or something, when all of a sudden Helen Vaughan says that raidworks continue to operate on the Rock Raid saithbaind between the Tara Hotel and the Punchbowl, and the Old Belgord Raid is claised to traffic immediately saith of the junction with Embankment Raid. Three goys in a silver Peugeot 206 pass me, roysh, and they all have a good scope into the cor, obviously thinking it's a bird driving it because it's, like, a bird's cor, I have to admit, I get that all the time, and when they see it's a goy they all, like, crack their shites laughing, roysh, so I just give them the finger.

I get home from town at, like, four o'clock in the afternoon, roysh, and the old man's standing in the hallway, totally white, and we're talking totally here. He goes, "Ross, you're home". I'm just there, "No shit, Sherlock" and he goes, "Come into the kitchen and sit down. I've got some bad news." I'm there, "What are you crapping on about". He goes, "They're moving the Irish rugby team, Ross. They're moving them to... God, I can't even say it... The northside. The northside, Ross... I'm sorry."

There's a smell of whiskey off his breath, roysh, and there's a huge whack gone out of the bottle of Jameson he got off his golfing mates for his 50th. He always tries to be real palsy-walsy with me when he's, like, pissed.

I'm, like, totally starving. I'm there, "Where's mum?" He's like, "Out. She has coffee every Thursday afternoon, with the girls. You know that." I'm like, "What's the story with dinner?" but he doesn't seem to, like, hear me. He goes, "I've been trying to catch her on her mobile since two o'clock, but of couse she's in the National Gallery, she's not going to have it on." I'm just there, "What's for dinner?" and he's like, "She's a strong woman, your mother. Heaven knows I need her now..."

I get up from the table, roysh, open the press and grab, like, three packets of Chipsticks and a handful of funsize Mars bars and I'm about to head up to my room, roysh, when the old man pours himself another drink, sits down at the table, puts his head in his hands and starts, like, bawling his eyes out, the sad bastard. I'm just there, "What is YOUR problem?" He goes, "Lansdowne Road, Ross. It's over." I'm there, "What part of the northside are we talking?" Oh my God he loses it then, roysh, he's like, "DOES IT MATTER?" and then, like, twenty seconds later he goes, "I'm sorry for flying off the handle, Ross. God knows, this isn't easy for any of us... For what it's worth, it's going to be a place called Abbotstown." I'm like, "Where the fock is Abbotstown?" I don't know why I'm actually bothering to sound interested. He's there, "A million miles away from the Berkeley Court basically. Two million miles from Kiely's." I'm like, "So what? The Dort goes there, I presume." He just, like, shakes his head and goes, "Think again, Ross." Then he knocks back his drink, roysh, and pours himself another, blubbering to himself, the total sap.

I open a Mars bar and pop it into my mouth and there's this, like, total silence between us. There's a bag on the table and I'm like, "What's this?" He doesn't answer. I open it and it's, like, a David Gray album. *White Ladder*. The old man comes out of his trance and he's like, "Oh that. It's some record that Sorcha lent to your mother." She's SO trying to get back with me it's not funny. He starts, like, dabbing at his eyes with a tissue and he's like, "Did I tell you we met her? In the Frascati Shopping Centre?" I'm like, "Yeah, only a thousand focking times". He goes, "He has a tremendous voice, that David Gray. Very unusual". I just, like, throw my eyes up to heaven, roysh, and pick up the new mobile phone catalogue I got in town? I'm thinking of getting a new one. Maybe the Motorola V3690. Maybe the Nokia 8850.

Then the old man starts up his bullshit again. He's like, "It's all about votes, Ross. Oh, you should have heard that blasted Bertie Ahern on the one o'clock news. So bloody smug. A national stadium. Quote-unquote. To boost his popularity out in – what's this you call it? – Knackeragua. A couple of the goys are coming around this evening. Basically we're going to set up a pressure group: KISS. Stands for Keep It South Side." I'm like, "You're focking pissed". He either doesn't hear me or decides to ignore me, roysh, because the next thing he's, like, up on his feet, pacing up and down the kitchen, practicing some speech which he says he's going to make tonight. He's there, "Think of the northside and you immediately think of unmarried mothers, council houses, coal sheds and curry sauce. You think of cannabis, lycra tracksuits and football jerseys worn as fashion garments. You think of Bob Marley blasting out on one of these fearful ghetto-busters, men with little moustaches selling *An Phoblacht* outside the social security office, mothers and fathers in the pub from morning till night, *Fair City*, entire families existing off welfare and, sadly, the twin scourges of drugs and satellite dishes." I'm like, "Sit down, you're making a complete orse of yourself", but he carries on, and he's there, "There are some people in this country who want our community to become a mirror of that. And that is why every white, Anglo-Saxon one of us has to stand up and treat this northside stadium nonsense as an attack on our way of life. Mark my words, this is just the thin end of the wedge. Next will be a methadone clinic in Foxrock..."

I hear the front door closing and it's, like, the old dear, roysh, and I'm just there, "Thank fock for that." But then, roysh, she bursts straight into the kitchen and she goes, "Charles, I came as soon as I heard" and the two of them start, like, hugging each other, complete knobs the two of them, him pissed off his face on whiskey, her doped off her head on, like, cappuccino? And they both TOTALLY blank me. And we are talking total here. She's like, "What are you going to do, Charles?" He's like, "We. What are WE going to do?" She's there, "Yes, of course. I'm with you, you know that." He goes, "I'm going to fight it. Basically some of the goys are coming over here tonight." She goes,

"I'm so proud of you.. AND... because I knew you'd need cheering up... guess what I bought?" She, like, pulls out a small Gloria Jeans bag, roysh, and sort of, like, dances it up and down in front of is eyes and she goes, "Your favourite, Charles. Colombia Narino supreme." He goes, "Yippee, I'll fill the percolator", and she goes, "WAIT....", roysh, and she pulls out this box from, like, Thorntons, and she's there, "Guess." Oh my God I feel like borfing? He has this stupid smile on his face, roysh, and he goes, "Are we talking cherry almond charlottes?" And she nods her head, roysh, and she's there, "AND? Walnut kirsch marzipan."

He gets out the cups. Two cups. He's like, "I thought I was losing my mind before you came home." And she goes, "Well I'm here now, Charles." He's like, "Sitting at the table, feeling sorry for myself." He takes a filter from the packet and then stops all of a sudden and he goes, "Oh my God, why didn't I think of it before? You are SUCH an inspiration, dorling." The old dear goes, "I know that look... You're going to write a letter to *The Irish Times*, aren't you?" And he's there, "You're damn right I am" and she goes, "I'll go and get your pen." I'm standing at the kitchen door, roysh, and the old dear brushes straight past me to go into the study and, like, doesn't say a word to me. The old man goes, "Get my good one, dorling. The Mont Blanc one."

The old dear comes back, roysh, and puts the pen and some of the old man's good writing paper on the table. He hands her a cup of coffee and he goes, "*The Irish Times* will be behind me. Hell, I might even get in touch with Gerry Thornley." She goes, "No, remember what the judge said, Charles. Two miles." He's there, "No, no, no. That'll all have been forgotten about by now... How was the gallery anyway?" She goes, "Oh, we went to the Westbury in the end. Change of scenery." They both sit down at the table and I just give them a filthy and go, "Fock's sake, you two are as sad as each other", and I head up to my room. The old dear shouts after me, "Don't go far, Ross. Dinner will be ready in an hour. It's soba noodles with chicken and ginger."

We're walking up Grafton Street, roysh, we're talking me, Oisínn and JP, and we're passing by Bewley's and this Romanian bird is standing outside selling *The Big Issue*. We walk past her, roysh, and she's like, "Big Issue, Big Issue", and JP turns around and he goes, "That's a nasty sneeze you've got there", and we all break our shites laughing.

❖   ❖   ❖   ❖   ❖

There was a huge row in the pub the other night, roysh. Erika was going on about the national lottery, which she said was basically for skangers and Claire – who basically IS a skanger, roysh, we're talking a Dalkey wannabe who actually lives in Bray – she goes, "But what about my mum? She buys scratch cards. That doesn't mean I'M a skanger." And Erika goes, "I'm not changing my theory to accommodate you, your mother or any member of your family. Scratch cards are no different from actually doing the lottery. They are SO working class it's not funny." And Claire starts going ballistic, roysh, screaming and shouting, telling her she's the biggest snob she's ever met, which Erika would actually consider a compliment, roysh, and Erika just smiles while Claire makes a total fool of herself and eventually Sorcha, my ex who's doing the DBS in Carysfort, she takes her off to the toilet to calm her down and, like, clean up her make-up and shit, which totally pisses Erika off, I can tell, because she looks at me and goes, "Sorry, whose best friend is that girl supposed to be again?" Then she gets up and leaves the pub without even finishing her Bacardi Breezer.

The next morning, roysh, I head out to Erika's gaff in Stillorgan, just to, like, tell her I thought she was actually in the right the night before and I thought she was really badly treated, blah blah blah, basically just trying to get in there. Her old dear answers the door, roysh, and she says she's not in, she's actually down with her horse, though I might be able to get her on her mobile if she has it switched on, but I tell her I'll, like, head down to the stables myself to see can I catch her.

When I see her, roysh, she's carrying this, like, bucket of I-don't-know-what, basically some type of shit she feeds the horses, and I'm straight over, playing the total gentleman, going, "Erika, let me carry that for you". When I go to take it from her, though, she shoots me this filthy, roysh, so I just hold my hands up and go, "Hey, no offence". I follow her into the stable and she puts the bucket down and then goes, "Your girlfriend has an attitude problem." I ask her who she means, roysh, and she goes, "Sorcha" and I tell her that Sorcha isn't my girlfriend, which she just, like, ignores. She's there, "I so love her little friend. The one with the Rimmel foundation. She made such an impression in The Queen's last night, didn't she? That's what you get when you go dredging for friends in Bray." I'm like, "That's actually what I'm here for, Erika..." She goes, "What are you here for, Ross?" I'm about to tell her that

16

I thought she got, like, the shitty end of the stick last night, roysh, when all of a sudden she goes, "Do you want to be with me? Is that why you're here?" And even though she makes it sound sort of, like, sleazy, roysh, I tell her yes and she goes, "Okay then, let's go".

So I just grab her, roysh, and we stort doing, like, tongue sarnies, and I have to say, even though the boots and the jodhpurs are a major turn-on, she's not actually as good a kisser as I remembered from the last time I was with her two years ago. I open my eyes a couple of times, sort of, like, mid-snog, roysh, and notice that she has her eyes open the whole time and this sort of sounds, like, weird, roysh, but it was like kissing a dead body and the only response I actually get out of her is when we, like, stumble backwards into the hay and I try to go a bit further than just snogging, you can't blame a goy for chancing his arm, and she just looks over my shoulder and goes, "Get off me. I have to feed Orchid."

Christian must have been out on the lash with a few of the goys last night because he stinks of Red Bull, roysh, and he only has one eyebrow. Fionn calls him the kangaroo court jester. It suddenly, like, dawns on me, roysh, that I've never actually seen Christian with a full set of eyebrows. This is how bored I am. I'm in sociology, roysh, and the lecturer's blabbing on about some bird called Emile Durkheim and I turn to Kelso – ex Michael's boy, sound though – and I'm like, "Are we in the right focking lecture hall?" He goes, "Amazingly, yes. Though what any of this shit has to do with sport I don't know."

The lecturer, I don't even know what his focking name is, he snares Kelso then, roysh, and he's like, "You up there. No, not you. Behind you. The boy with the blue and white striped shirt." Kelso's there, "Me?" The goy's like, "Yes, you. Would you like to come down and talk to us about dialectical materialism?" And Kelso goes, "Eh, no". The goy's there, "Okay, we'll cut a deal then, I'll stay down here talking to the class about Emile Durkheim and you stay up there with your mouth shut." I turn around to Kelso and I'm like, "Sorry, man", and he goes, "It's cool".

Oisínn looks as though he's in, like, a trance, just staring down at the ground, roysh, but then my mobile phone beeps and I notice that he's sent me a text message and it's, like, a Limerick, roysh, and it's like, "THERE WAS A YOUNG ROCK BOY NAMED ROSS, WHOSE LIFE WAS A BIT OF A DOSS, UNMATCHED WAS HIS UNDIZZINESS, BUT HIS DAD OWNS A BUSI-

NESS, AND ONE DAY HE'LL MAKE ROSS THE BOSS." I'm about to send him one back, roysh, but he's, like, really good at them, and I can't think of any words that rhyme with Oisínn, so I just send him back a message and it's like, "RETARD!"

After the lecture, roysh, Christian comes over and he goes, "Hey Padwan, what the fock is sociology anyway?" I'm like, "Don't ask me. I thought it was, like, the mind and shit." We decide to hit the bor, roysh, where we meet Fionn, who's doing Orts, we're talking psychology and Arabic, we're talking brains to focking burn here, and says he got the new U2 album. I ask him whether it's, like, as good as the first one and Oisínn butts in and says, yeah, it's WAY better than *Pop*.

We're standing in the queue to get into the nightclub, roysh, and the girls are giving the bouncers loads, it's all, "Hi, honey" and "Oh-my-God how-are-you?" and hugs and air-kisses all round. They're on, like, first name terms with every single one of the doormen, not because they actually like them, roysh – they don't, most bouncers are basically skangers who'd be turned away from basically any half-decent nightclub on their night off – but the girls, they actually make it their business to find out their names, and then they go up to the door and start, like, flirting their orses off, hugging them and going, "You weren't here last week. Oh my God, I really missed you", and it's all kisses on the cheek, or in Emer's case, and in Chloë's as well, on the lips. And all because they're shit-scared of being asked for ID or getting, like, turned away. Of course the bouncers haven't a clue what any of the girls' names are. One bird in a short skirt and a pink titty-top is basically the same as the next and these goys are, like, you know, getting their jollies off fifty or sixty birds a night, they don't care, it's one of the perks of the job. So everyone's getting something out of it. Fionn explained it to me. He said it was a contract of mutual convenience or some shit. And then when we go up to the door they stort giving us focking daggers. It's like, "Where are you coming from lads?" And we go, the Bailey, the M1, Kiely's, whatever. And they're like, "It's regulars only tonight." And the girls come out and go, "It's okay, goys, they're with us", and they let us in and tell us to behave ourselves. And, like, we're actually supposed to be grateful.

Pretty much the only part of freshers' day I can remember, roysh, is chatting to these two Mounties in some focking marquee or other, having drunk, like, ten pints of Heino, which is the only beer they were selling on the day. I remember the birds coming up to us, we're talking me, Christian, Oisínn and Eanna, and one of them, roysh, I think she's first year Social Science, she goes, "Oh my God did you hear about Becky?" I went, "No, what's the story?" sort of, like, hiding the fact that I didn't have a focking clue who Becky was. She goes, "Oh my God she drank half a bottle of vodka straight. She had to be brought home in an ambulance. Her mum is so going to have a knicker fit."

I don't actually remember when these two birds focked off, roysh, but I'm sort of, like, vaguely aware that either Oisínn and Eanna said something totally out of order to one of them and then the next hour is sort of, like, a blur. I fell asleep at one stage, with my feet up on the chair opposite me and then I woke up maybe half an hour later with all, like, spit dribbling down my chin and this bird who I've never laid eyes on before sitting beside me, boring the ears off me about some bullshit or other. She was actually talking about some cousin of hers, roysh, who also went to Castlerock and she was wondering whether I, like, knew him. I remember asking her how she knew what school I went to and she went, "HELLO? Your jersey?" and I'd actually forgotten that we'd all worn our Castlerock jerseys for the day, roysh, I mean we focking had to because we heard that all the goys from Gonzaga were wearing theirs, and Michael's, Blackrock, the Gick, everyone.

So anyway, roysh, this bird, it turns out her name's Jade, she had my mobile at one stage and she was, like, flicking through my phone book on it, going, "Keyser? Is that Dermot Keyes? Oh my God I can't believe you know Dermot Keyes. I was going to bring him to my debs." Then it's like, "Oh my God, you know Eanna Fallon. I kissed his best friend in Wesley when I was, like, fourteen. Oh my God that's so embarrassing." I was sort of, like, aware that this went on for quite a while, roysh, even though I conked out after about, like, five minutes? I don't know what the fock happened then because the next thing I remember is she's, like, bawling her eyes out and she's asking me whether I think she's fat, but all I can see is Christian across the far side of the bar and he's, like, calling me, and I'm sort of, like, vaguely aware of some plan we had to rob this, like, ten-foot tall inflatable Heineken can from outside the student bor and hang it off the bridge over the dual carriageway. So I just, like, leave your one, roysh, and the next thing, me, Christian, Oisínn, Eanna and, I'm pretty sure Fionn, are trying to smuggle this, like, massive blow-up can out of UCD, trying to avoid the security goys who were, like, driving around in jeeps and shit.

And the next thing I remember after that, roysh, is the cops asking me for my name, my address and my number. I don't know where the rest of the goys focked off to, but I'm, like, instantly sober now, and obviously, roysh, I don't want my parents to know that I focked this thing over the bridge and onto the dual carriageway, so I give them my name and Sorcha's address and phone number, because I know she's actually the only one in her house at the moment, her parents and her sister are in, like, the south of France. Anyway, roysh, they bring me to Donnybrook and this complete focking bogger of a cop takes my details and then tells me to turn out my pockets and hand over my belt and shoelaces. I'm like, "Why do you need those?" and he goes, "Because you're going to be placed in a cell". I'm like, "Duh, no shit, Sherlock. I know THAT. What the fock do you want my shoelaces for?" He's there, "In case you try to hang yourself". I'm like, "Hang myself? Whoah, who the fock owned that Heineken can? Is there something I should know here?" He tells me I have a big mouth that's going to get me into trouble and I'm like, "Spare me".

So eventually Sorcha arrives at the cop shop to collect me, roysh, although she takes, like, two focking hours to get there and when they finally let me out of the focking cell I can see why. She's, like, totally dressed to kill, the sad bitch. She's wearing the Burberry cognac leather knee-high boots her old dear bought her in New York, her long black Prada skirt, her black cashmere turtle neck sweater by Calvin Klein and her sleeveless, faux sheepskin jacket by Karen Millen. As if I'm supposed to believe she always looks this well at, like, three o'clock in the morning. I was SO glad to see her though and I gave her a hug and tried to kiss her but she, like, pulled away from me, roysh, and I'm just there going, 'Oh my God this one is in a fouler now'.

The cops decided not to charge me, roysh, but they said they'd, like, keep the incident on file and if I'm ever arrested again, blah, blah, blah. They give me my shit back, but I'm still too off-my-face to, like, put my shoelaces back into my shoes, roysh, so I just stuff them into my pocket and walk out the door, while Sorcha spends about ten focking minutes apologising to the cops for my behaviour, totally overdoing it with the mature young adult act, and we're talking totally here.

We get into her cor, roysh – black Rav 4, we're talking totally amazing here – and the nagging storts straight away. She's like, "Your first day at college, Ross. It was certainly one to remember, wasn't it?" I just, like, totally blank her, which really pisses her off. She goes, "Don't worry, you'll grow out of it". On the other side of the road, there was, like, two or three buses turning into the bus depot in Donnybrook and I realised that it was actually a lot earlier than I thought it was. Sorcha goes, "By the way, that was a stupid thing you did back there. In the police station." I'm like, "What?" She goes, "Trying to kiss me... You TOLD them I was your sister." I'm like, "Oh well, you know what they say. Incest is best." She goes, "You owe me. BIG time." I'm like, "What do you mean, owe you?" She goes, "HELLO? Do you think I've nothing better to be doing than driving all the way from Killiney into town to get you out of a police cell." I'm there, "What were you doing when the cops called?" She looks at me, shakes her head and goes, "I HAVE a life, you know", which means she was actually doing fock-all.

I spent what seemed like the next hour falling in and out of sleep, roysh, but it must have only been a few minutes, because when I opened my eyes we were only at, like, the Stillorgan crossroads, and I realised that it was actually Sorcha's shouting which woke me up. I kept sort of belching and there was, like, baby sick on my chin and my jacket and Sorcha was going, "If you borf in my car, Ross, I am SO going to kill you". I wipe my face on my sleeve, tell her I love her when she's angry and go to kiss her on the cheek, but she tells me if I even think about it she'll break my arm. After a few minutes, roysh, completely out of the blue, she goes, "I'm seeing someone". She was, like, dying for me to ask who, roysh, but I didn't say anything and after a couple of minutes she went, "He's in my class. He's actually 28. The goys in Carysfort are SO much more mature than the goys in UCD."

She takes the right turn at White's Cross and she's there going, "I am SO over you, Ross. I look back now and I'm like, Oh my God, what a mistake." I don't say anything. She goes, "I mean, is the proposition of monogamy such a Jurassic notion to you?" Straight away, roysh, I recognise this as a line from *Dawson's Creek* and I'm just like, "Okay, Joey", and she realises that I'm not as pissed as she thought I was and she just goes really red and doesn't, like, say anything else for ages? I was, like, totally laughing my orse off.

She turned up the CD then, roysh, and I hadn't even, like, realised that she had it on. I was just like, "What is this shit?" and she throws her eyes up to heaven and goes, "It's Tchaikovsky, Ross. *Dance of the Reed Flute*? It's from *The Nutcracker*. Oh my God, Ross, when are you EVER going to get with the programme?" The cover from the CD was on the dashboard, roysh, and it was like, *The Best Classical Album of the Millennium... Ever!* I turned up the sound really high, roysh, until it was blasting, and then storted, like, conducting the music, swinging my arms around the place and Sorcha went, "You are SUCH a dickhead". We pulled up outside my gaff and I got out of the car and, like, staggered up to the gates of the house, and I must have left the passenger door open because I heard Sorcha getting out of the car and, like, cursing me under her breath, then slamming the door shut, and the next thing I knew I was waking up and it was, like, the middle of the afternoon the next day, and I still had my jersey and my chinos on and I was in the total horrors.

Me and Christian, we skip our eleven o'clock, roysh, and we're sitting in his gaff watching the telly when my mobile rings and I, like, make the mistake of answering before checking who it is. And who is it only the old man, roysh, obviously checking up on me. I'm there, "Not a good time, Dad. I'm watching *The Love Boat*," and I hang up.

I phone Erika up, roysh, on her mobile, and ask her where she is but she doesn't answer, just goes, "What do you want?" So I, like, get straight to the point. I'm there, "I just wanted to talk to you about, you know, what happened between us". She goes, "Make it quick. I'm in Nine West." I'm like, "Well, I just wanted to let you know that basically I won't say anything to Sorcha. About, you know, me and you being with each other. I know she's your best friend." And there's this, like, silence on the other end of the line. I'm there, "Are you still there?" She goes, "The line is perfect, Ross. Is that all you want to say?" and I'm like, "Well, I just wondered whether you were going to say anything to her." And she goes, "You have major problems, Ross. Do you think being with you is something I'd ACTUALLY brag about?"

# Chapter Two

## The one where Ross has a mare of a christmas

I ask for a large latte, roysh, and the bird behind the counter, who's, like, French or some shit, she says they have no large, so I ask for a small instead and she goes, "No small". I'm like, "What HAVE you focking got?" She goes, "Only grande, tall and short". And at this stage, roysh, I'm so confused I don't know what the fock to ask for, so I head back to Melissa to see whether it's going to be tall or short, roysh, and she just, like, looks me up and down, roysh, and goes, "Will you GROW up. This is focking serious", and for a couple of seconds I think she's talking about the coffee, roysh, but as she stands up and, like storms out of the place I finally cop that she's actually talking about what happened at the Orts Ball, or should I say afterwards.

I leg it after her, roysh, but she's already across the other side of the road, up by the Central Bank, and the lights are red, but I leg it across anyway, and this spa in a blue Nissan Almera beeps me, roysh, and I just, like, give him the finger. I catch up with Melissa and, like, touch her on the shoulder, but she just, like, spins around and goes, "Nicole was SO right about you". I'm going, "Who the fock is Nicole?" and she's there, "You are SUCH an asshole. That's what she told me, Ross. And she was right." I'm like, "Hey, I said I'd meet you this morning and I did." She goes, "You just want to make sure I go through with it". I'm there, "No, I wanted to be here with you. This is something you shouldn't have to go through on your own." She goes, "You are SO full of shit. You're just thinking about what your parents would say if they found out I was..." I'm like, "Bullshit. Anyway, you're not", and she turns around and starts walking again, off through Temple Bar, and I follow her from, like, a safe distance.

There's a goy busking in the archway outside Abrakebabra, roysh, and it's like, 'Don't Look Back In Anger', and as we're waiting for the lights, roysh, I tell Melissa that that song has been SO ruined by every focking busker in town playing it, but she just ignores me, as she does when I ask her why they're building a new bridge next to the Ha'penny Bridge. She just, like, shakes her head, roysh, and I am SO tempted to point out that this is only, like, fifty percent my fault, that it takes, like, two to tango. But it'll only make things worse.

The place is next door to Pravda, roysh, and Melissa presses the button on the intercom and says she has an appointment and the next thing, roysh, we're standing at a desk and the woman asks her whether she's attended the clinic before and Melissa, like, she looks your one up and down and goes, "Hordly". The next thing, roysh, we're sitting down in the waiting room and Melissa's filling out this, like, form and she gives it to the nurse and then we just, like, sit there and wait, in total silence. I sort of look sideways at her a couple of times, roysh, and I have to say she's actually a bit better looking that I thought she was last night. She looks a little bit like Charisma Carpenter, except with blonde hair. I only ended up with her because Christian wanted to be with her best friend, Stephanie, who actually does look like Natalie Portman, and he asked me to take a bullet for him, which, being the great mate that I am, I did. They're both, like, first year Orts.

Eventually, roysh, the doctor calls her into his office and I'm not sure whether I'm supposed to, like, go in with her, but as I go to stand up Melissa tells me to sit and mind her stuff, which suits me fine. I'm sitting there, roysh, looking around and there's, like, a girl sitting two seats down from me who I think I recognise from Anabel's, and she's, like, a nervous wreck, can't stop fidgeting. And all of a sudden, roysh, Melissa's phone storts beeping, so I grab it out of her bag and notice that she has a text message from some bird called Gwen and it's like, "OMG", which I presume means Oh My God, "DAWSON & PACEY R BCK TALKNG". I just flick through all her numbers, roysh, and I notice that she knows two or three girls I've actually been with before, but I still don't have a clue who Gwen is and I think about writing her number down but in the end I don't bother.

I put her phone back in her bag, roysh, and stort flicking through a copy of *Now!* magazine which the girl two seats down has just put back on the coffee table and I stort reading an interview with Beyonce from Destiny's Child, who says that it's her mother who actually styles the band, and an article about how you can achieve the Liz Hurley look by using this gel, roysh, lactic acid or some shit, to increase the flow of blood to the lips, making them look fuller, which sorts of sounds, like, weird to me.

About ten minutes later, roysh, Melissa comes out and it's all, like, thank-you this and thank-you that to the doctor, but her face changes when she sees me and she just, like, heads straight for the door and I follow her down the stairs. We head back towards Grafton Street and, even though I have no interest in seeing her again, I ask her what she's doing later and she goes, "Leaning over the toilet and getting sick, I would imagine." I ask her what she's talking about and she goes, "Do you have ANY idea what I've just taken?" and I'm like, "The morning-after pill?" and she just shakes her head and tells me I haven't got a clue. She says she's going down for the Dort, roysh, and I tell her I'm going to get the 46A. And I don't know why, maybe because I feel sorry for her, I ask her whether I'll see her in college tomorrow and she tells me not to get my hopes up, that she's seeing someone.

The clerk of the court, roysh, he takes the hospital report from this complete focking skanger in the witness box, roysh, we're talking total trailer park trash here, and he hands it to Judge Judy, roysh, and Christian goes, "That goy has got the best job in the world". He shakes his head and he's like, "Bet he can't believe his luck." I'm there, "What are you talking about?" He goes, "Just imagine, roysh, if all you had to do all day was sit around and watch Judge Judy in action." And we look at each other, roysh, stort breaking our orses laughing and then, like, high-five each other.

I'm like, "She's one tough lady". He's there, "She dispenses justice with an iron fist, Ross. An iron fist." I'm like, "Do you know who would make a really good Judge Judy if they ever did it in England?" He thinks for a few seconds, roysh, and then we both go at the same time, "Anne Robinson".

Christian goes, "Oh my God, you're right. She would SO rock. THE PLANTIFF IS THE WEAKEST LINK GOODBYE!"

I go out to the kitchen and put another packet of popcorn into the microwave. I have to say I never thought I'd learn so much in the first few months of college. Judge Judy throws out the goy's compensation claim and Christian says he's going to stort using the word baloney a lot more in conversation.

I'm on the Rock Road and I am SO pissed off it's unbelievable, roysh, because this total asshole in a blue Ford Escort in front of me has decided he needs focking petrol, roysh, and he's waiting to turn right across, like, a whole lane of traffic to get to the petrol station, but of course the traffic is, like, bomper to bomper coming the other way and no one will let him through, which means I'm stuck behind the focker and I'm too far up his orse to actually slip into the slow lane, so I'm focking stuck. But FINALLY someone lets him across, roysh, and I'm like hoo-focking-ray, and I'm halfway down the road when some bitch overtakes me on the inside lane in a black Seat Ibiza.

I was seeing this girl for about three weeks, roysh, Georgia's her name and she was, like, one of the weather girls on Network Two, total stunner, SO like Laetitia Casta it's unbelievable, but thick as a focking brick and we are talking total here. We were in Anabel's one night, roysh, and we're sitting with Barser and Eddie, these two heads I knew from Castlerock, doing politics or some shit, TOTAL focking brainboxes, not really into rugby but, like, sound anyway. So the Nice Treaty comes up in conversation, roysh, and I have to say I know fock-all about Northern Ireland, but I do know to keep my mouth shut in case I, like, embarrass myself and shit. Georgia, of course, doesn't. She goes, "Oh my God, I am SO sick of all these, like, referendums and stuff. I don't know why they can't just rip up the Constitution and just have one article, which says, like, you know, 'WHATever'." And the goys, roysh, fair play to them, they just storted, like, nodding their heads, as though she'd made an amazing point, but I could tell, roysh, they were looking at her going, 'What the fock is Ross going out with?'

I had started to ask myself the same question – Oisínn and Fionn, roysh, they call her Clueless – and I was seriously thinking about giving her the flick this night in Anabel's, roysh, having done the dirt on her about three days before that with Heidi, this bird who's, like, deputy head girl in Killiney. Anyway, roysh, I didn't have the heart to do it because, as it turned out, RTE had, like, given her the boot that day, for what I don't know, because I was pretty shit-faced when she explained it to me and I really couldn't have been orsed listening, even though she was, like, bawling her eyes out.

Of course, coming up to the end of the night, roysh, it doesn't look like I'm going to get my shift anywhere else, so I start, like pretending to be all concerned, giving her all, like, hugs and kisses and shit, and going, "They must be mad letting you go" – she probably stuck a focking rain cloud on the map upside down or something – "they'll regret that one day. You'll be the star they let slip through their fingers." And she goes, "HELLO? I have a degree in communications from ATIM, Ross. I'm HORDLY likely to walk into another job." I'm like, "With your looks?" and I know straight away that I've said the wrong thing, roysh, and she gives me this total filthy and goes, "You think I'm an airhead, don't you? Good-looking with nothing between my ears." And the tears start again. I stort going, "Of course I don't", but I'm struggling to keep a straight face, roysh, because I can hear all the goys – we're talking Christian, Fionn, JP – and they're all totally ripping the piss, shouting over, "Tomorrow will be a clidey day" and "there'll be scashered shars throughout the country", like they always do, roysh, and I'm caught between wanting to look all, like, sympathetic to make sure I get my bit later on, while at the same time playing Jack the Lad in front of the goys, letting them think I'm actually ripping the piss out of her myself. It's a focking tightrope, but I manage not to burst out laughing in her face and all of a sudden, roysh, a couple of her mates arrive over – birds she knows from Mount Anville, JP was with one of them once – and they take her off to the toilets.

Oisínn comes over and high-fives me, roysh, and asks whether I heard about Eanna and I tell him no and he goes, "You will never guess who he copped off with." I'm like, "Who?" And he goes, "Anais Anais." I'm not sure whether it's because he's just, like, bad with names, roysh, but Oisínn always refers to girls by their smell. I don't know who the fock he's talking about, but I think it might be Olwen Patten, this total stunner who's, like, repeating in the Institute, and who Eanna was talking to up at the bor at the stort of the night. I'm like, "Cool." Oisínn, who's completely off his tits drunk, roysh, he goes, "Where's the focking weather girl?" I'm like, "Toilets" He goes, "What was all that crying about? Did she find out about..." I'm like, "No, no. RTE gave her the flick today." He nods sort of, like, thoughtfully, roysh, even though he hasn't really got a clue what I said, the music is so loud, and he goes, "Bummer" and I'm there, "Total."

'Shackles' comes on, roysh, and Fionn and JP are giving it loads out on the dancefloor and they give me the old thumbs up, roysh, and I do it back and I can see Christian chatting up some bird I know to see from the M1 and he's no doubt telling her that, I don't know, that he senses a strange disturbance in the Force, which is his usual chat-up line, roysh, because she's sort of, like, leaning away from him, as though he's completely off his focking rocker, which he actually is. The next thing I know, Georgia's back from the toilets and she's, like, tied her cardigan around her waist, roysh, and she's wearing this halter-neck top, which is pretty revealing and it's only when she goes, "Do you want to stay in Ailish's house with me? Her parents are in Bologna", that I realise she's a lot more pissed than I actually thought and I tell her I'll go and get my jacket. I know I was going to give her the flick, roysh, but, as Oisínn always says, you don't put three weeks of spadework into a job and then give up when the treasure's in sight. I knock back the rest of my pint, roysh, and I look up and – OH MY FOCKING GOD – you will not believe who was standing next to Georgia, only Heidi, roysh, and I'm just there going, 'How the FOCK am I going to get out of this one?'

Heidi goes, "Hi, Ross." And Georgia, roysh, sensing another bird moving in on her patch, she sits beside me, or sort of, like, flops down on the couch, and links my orm, and Heidi, roysh, who's actually looking really well, a bit like Yasmine Bleeth, except thinner, she goes, "Oh, I see you've moved on, Ross." I have to say, roysh, I'm, like, so pissed at this stage, I can hordly string a sentence together and I go, "That's right, Heidi. Onwards and upwards." She looks Georgia up and down, roysh, and she goes, "I'd HORDLY call that upwards." And Georgia, roysh, she turns around to me and she goes, "Sorry, who is this... girl?"

And Heidi, roysh, who's, like, well able for her, fair play to her, she goes, "My name is Heidi. And I know who you are." Georgia goes, "Oh, I recognise you now. Collars up, knickers down." And Heidi's like, "Better than Mount Anything." Georgia's there, "You're in Emma's class, my little sister", trying to put her down like, making out she's only a kid or something, but Heidi's there, "Your sister is a knob, just like you". Georgia stands up, roysh, and she goes, "My sister is NOT a focking knob", and Heidi laughs, roysh, shakes her head and goes, "Oh my God she's not even allowed to do supervised study".

At this stage, roysh, it looks like it's going to get ugly, so I go to get up to get another pint in, maybe find the lads, and Heidi all of a sudden goes, "Ross obviously hasn't told you about us, has he?" I'm like, 'Oh shit'. Georgia goes, "I'm not interested in whatever mistakes Ross might have made in the distant past." And Heidi's like, "Distant past? Try Wednesday night." And the next thing, roysh, Georgia, oh my God, she picks up a bottle of Coors Light and, like, pours the whole thing over my focking head, then runs out of the place bawling her eyes out. Heidi focks off as well, laughing her head off. One of

Georgia's mates, roysh – not the one JP was with, the other one, I think she's doing Tourism Management and Marketing in LSB – she comes over and tells me I'm an asshole. I'm like, "I wasn't going out with Georgia, you know. We were only seeing each other." And she looks at me really, like, coldly, roysh, and goes, "Asshole."

I sit there for a few minutes, completely focking soaked, just knowing that my new light blue Ralph is going to stink of beer for ages, and I'm sort of thinking about maybe heading to the jacks to stick it under the drier and then going off looking for Heidi, but I'm so off-my-face at this stage I really couldn't be orsed. I can't actually remember how long I'm sitting there when all of a sudden Fionn comes over, roysh, and sits down next to me and he goes, "What the fock happened?" I'm like, "Georgia found out about Heidi." He goes, "Heidi's the one you were with in..." I'm like, "The Club on Wednesday night." Fionn goes, "Well, you were going to give Georgia the flick anyway, weren't you?" I'm like, "Yeah, totally." And he goes, "Well then... Every clide has a silver lining".

I send Erika a text message, roysh, and it's like, "w%d U lIk 2go4 a drink?" and straight away I get one back and it's like, "GAL", which I presume stands for get a life, because that's what she always says. She actually says it to everyone. It's like, "GET a life".

Zoey hates Aoife. According to Fionn, who has been with both of them, Zoey is pretty much anorexic, roysh, while Aoife is, like, bulimic and, according to his theory, which he says is backed up by some of the world's leading psychologists, girls with anorexia look down on girls with bulimia, because they've got no willpower, roysh, and girls with bulimia hate girls who are, like, anorexic because they have got willpower. But Zoey, roysh, she says it's because Aoife has an attitude problem, a serious attitude problem, and because last week she told her to wear her black and silver, high-heeled, leather slingbacks, the Karen Millen ones, with beige suedette trousers she got from Joseph, knowing full well that they wouldn't go together and just saying it to be a bitch, as if she can afford to be after what she wore to the

Comm Ball. She says all this to me when I meet her in the queue in 911 – she's buying a packet of popcorn and a bottle of water – and she asks me whether I'm training this afternoon. I tell her no, I've pretty much decided to take it easy this year on the rugby front, haven't really bothered my orse going to training, just decided to pretty much doss for the year. She doesn't, like, react to this one way or the other, just tells me she was in Lillies on Saturday night and I ask her was anyone in there and she says no, unless of course you'd call Lorraine Keane and one of the Carter Twins someone.

I get this text message from Georgia and it's like, "WE REGRET TO INFORM OUR CUSTOMERS THAT THE EIRCELL NETWORK HAS GONE DOWN. HOWEVER THIS WILL NOT AFFECT YOU. NOT EVEN A NET-WORK WOULD GO DOWN ON YOU." Oh my God she is turning out to be SUCH a bunny boiler. I'm just like, you know, get over it, girl.

The big day finally arrived – the tension, the butterflies, all the goys gee-ing me up, the old pair finally getting off my case about not going to lectures and shit. It was, like, the finals of the Dublin Bus Most Irritating Mobile Phone User on Public Transport awards and they were on in the Berkeley Court. I was nominated in the 'Most Irritating Ringtone on the 46A' category for 'The Hairs on her Dickie-Die-Doh', which I downloaded off the internet in the computer room, roysh, and I was also an outsider for the 'Most Obnox-ious Mobile Phone User on Public Transport Anywhere' award, which is the award that everyone wants to win, so I was, like, really excited.

The whole thing was, like, a black tie affair, roysh, with the presentations made by Denis with one n O'Brien, who gave this amazing speech at the start and it was like, "When mobile phones first came out, people found it quite embarrassing if they had one that rang while they were on a bus or train. Invariably, all you would hear from them would be a muffled, 'I'm on the bus. I'll call you back', before they would switch it off and continue to stare, red-faced, out of the window. Now, we have a more confident, go-getting genera-tion of young people who know no embarrassment. They are not only talking on their mobile phones, but talking loudly and obnoxiously, actually making calls themselves, sending text messages without lowering the beep and generally making public transport journeys a miserable experience for hundreds of thousands of commuters every day of the week. And that is what we are here to acknowledge tonight."

I had, like, a lump in my throat. The first award, roysh – the 'Most Obnoxious Newcomer' award – went to seven-year-old Cameron Hewson from Willow Pork, whose old dear bought him a Nokia 8850 – we're talking dual band, data compatible, 36 ringtones and 300 minutes of battery talktime – just in case the traffic on the Rock Road was really heavy, roysh, and she had to tell him she'd be late picking him up from school.

The 'Most Annoying Way to Answer a Mobile Phone' award was a total steal for 17-year-old Fiona with a *fada* Clarke, who's, like, sixth year in Muckross. She was on her way to school, roysh, when her friend Neve rang to ask whether she was on the 46A on the front of her or the one behind her, and she answered the phone – a basic 087 Ready-to-Go – with a "Y'ello" and then continued to conduct her conversation at a decibel level estimated by the judges to be similar to that of a small plane taking off.

Then they moved on through the various 'Most Irritating Ringtone' awards, roysh, and the competition was really stiff in the classical music section. This spa from Michael's eventually won it for the *William Tell Overture*, roysh, seeing off the challenge from classics such as *Eine Kleine Nachtmusik*, *The Blue Danube*, *Für Elise* and 'Mozart 40', thanks mainly to the fact that he let the ring go on for about sixty seconds on the Dort one morning before finally answering it. "Tiernan managed to irritate a carriage-load of commuters while running the considerable risk of having his phone shoved – handset, facia, aerial and all – up his arse," his citation read. "His bravery must be commended."

The Country and Western section was also majorly tight, with *Home on the Range* the narrow favourite to win it for 16-year-old Jamie Sullivan from Gonzaga, but he ended up being beaten, roysh, by a total outsider, some dickhead from Clongowes who managed to, like, download *Help Me Make It Through The Night* onto his phone from a Kris Kristofferson website.

Then came the moment I'd been waiting for, roysh – the award for 'Most Irritating Ringtone on the 46A'. And... Yyyeeesss!!! I won it. Oh my God I couldn't believe it when Denis O'Brien read out my name. The judges mentioned the originality, obnoxiousness and high annoyance factor of *The Hairs on her Dicky-Die-Doh*, as I faced down competition from all-time commuter favourites such as *Popeye the Sailorman, La Marseillaise, Samba, Fuca* and *Jingle Bells.*

In my speech, roysh, I thanked Motorola for being brave enough to produce the Timeport 250, the latest tri-band handset with vibration alert and 140 hours of battery standby, without which I wouldn't be here. The award also wouldn't have been possible, I said, were it not for my old pair, who refuse to buy me a cor and there's, like, no way I'm turning up to college in the old dear's Micra, and the goys – namely Christian, Oisínn, Fionn and JP – for always ringing me when I'm on, like, the bus.

Unfortunately, I couldn't make it a double. The 'Most Obnoxious Mobile Phone User on Public Transport Anywhere' award went to Jonathon Thompson who's, like, fifth year Terenure College. He won it for spending 25 minutes texting one of his friends on the Dort, with the volume up full, then phoning his friend straight away to check whether he'd got it. He couldn't actually make the ceremony, roysh, but made his acceptance speech via a video link-up to, like, Blackrock Clinic, where surgeons spent four hours trying to remove his Siemens SL45 from his throat and oh my God my dreams are becoming so weird I am SO going to have to stop mixing my drinks.

Sophie rings me, roysh, to tell me that she's going to be late because there's, like, a signal failure on the Dorsh AGAIN and oh my God it's taken her, like, an hour to get from Glenageary to, like, Booterstown . She goes, "The Dorsh is a jake, Ross. A complete jake."

Emer's parents' house is worth over a million pounds, roysh, or so she tells us, but Sophie says that that is nothing because there's council houses, ACTUAL council houses, in Sallynoggin, we're talking Sally-focking-noggin here, which are going for two hundred grand. All of the girls go, "Oh my God", and all of the goys go, "Crazy shit", except me because I'm only sort of, like, half-listening. Erika is sitting opposite me, roysh, and she's looking pretty amazing I have to say, with that, like, permanent scowl on her face, or that's what Fionn calls it. I sent her a text message the other night and it was like, "U R my fantaC. C U l8r", but she didn't answer it and now I'm trying to, like, catch her eye, roysh, maybe wink at her across the table or blow her a kiss, something stupid just to say, you know, 'Our little secret' or whatever, but she's, like, totally ignoring the fact that I'm there. And when she finally does look at me, roysh, at the top of her voice she goes, "Ross, why are you staring at me?" and I can feel myself go puce and Sorcha, roysh, my ex who's doing the DBS in Carysfort, she starts staring at me, sort of, like, suspiciously. We're talking really pissed off that I might fancy her best friend. She takes off her scrunchy, slips it onto her wrist, shakes her hair free, smoothes it back into a low ponytail again, puts it back in the scrunchy and then, like, pulls five or six strands of hair loose again, then goes, "Ignore him, Erika. He's a weirdo." And Erika's there, "A MAJOR weirdo".

All the goys are cracking their shites laughing, roysh, I can hear them, and I'm, like, so focking morto that I don't know where to put myself, but Sophie sort of, like, rescues me by changing the subject and she goes, "It's a pity you can't buy, like, a glass of boiling water in a pub". And Emer's there, "Oh my God, that reminds me, how many points is a muffin?" and Sophie's like, "Five-and-a-half." And Emer goes, "There's no way that muffin was five-and-a-half." Sophie goes, "Emer, it was an American-style muffin and an American-style muffin is five-and-a-half points. I told you you shouldn't have had it, so don't take it out on me." Emer just gives her daggers.

Fionn turns around to me, roysh, and he goes, "Girls are obsessed with points, aren't they. When we were doing the Leaving it was getting as many as possible and now it's eating as few as possible", and I can feel another one of his theories coming on. Christian is, like, really quiet, roysh and I ask him if he's alright and he says he's cool. He's really knocking back the beers, though.

The girls are talking about some bird called Rachael who was in Loreto Foxrock and has put on SO much weight since she went on the pill and then they're talking about this big night out they have planned, where they're going to see Vonda Sheppard, a girls' night out, even though Sophie thinks her latest album SO isn't as good as her last one. And Sorcha says she wouldn't know because she's been listening to mostly classical music lately, especially Elgar's *Third Movement from Cello Concerto in E Minor Op 85*. Emer goes, "Oh my God, have you got *The Best Classical Album of the Millennium... Ever?*" and Sorcha, roysh, she goes, "Yeah, but I've got, like, loads of other classical albums as well that", really, like, defensive all of a sudden And Fionn goes, "You've probably got *The Best Classical Album of the Millennium... Ever Two, Three, Four* and *Five*, have you?" and I high-five him, even though I have to be honest, I don't really get the joke. Sophie says she loves that Pachelbel's *Canon* and Sorcha says she loves Rachmaninov's *Variation 18 from Rhapsody on a Theme by Paganini.*

And this pretty much goes on until Fionn asks whether we're going to The Vatican or not and we all grab our jackets and start heading up towards, like, Harcourt Street. We're pretty much halfway there, roysh, and me and Fionn are walking ahead of everyone basically talking rugby, Ireland's chances in the Six Nations, whether I could be as good as Brian O'Driscoll if I got my finger out, all that, when all of a sudden Sorcha shouts up to me, "Ross, where's Christian?" and I turn back, roysh, and I go, "I presumed he was with you lot." She's there, "No, he was behind us". I tell them all to walk on up, roysh, and I head back towards Grafton Street and I find him outside Planet Holywood, arguing with the bouncers. They've got, like, whatever they're focking called, C3PO and R2D2, in the window, roysh, and Christian, who's off his face, he wants to go in and touch the two robots, to see if they're, like, the real ones, the ones they used in the movie, which Christian reckons they're not, but the bouncers are not surprisingly having none of it, they're trying to move him along, and all of a sudden he storts going ballistic at them, going, "YOU DON'T OWN THEM. THEY BELONG TO THE PEOPLE."

I grab him, roysh, and sort of, like, drag up the street, but we only get, like, ten steps up the road when all of a sudden he stops and storts crying his eyes out and I keep asking him what's wrong, roysh, but he's too upset to talk and he just grabs me and hugs me there on the street and I'm sort of, like, you know, looking around to see who's, like, watching. I'm like, "What's wrong, Christian?" and he squeezes me horder, roysh, and I can hordly breathe at this stage, and I'm like, "What is it?" He goes, "My parents are getting a divorce." We just stand there looking at each other for ages, roysh, and I can't think of anything to say to him, even though he's been my best friend since we were, like, four, and I just end up going, "That is heavy shit, man." And he's crying, still holding onto me for dear life, and he goes, "When I was eight, my daddy rented out all of the *Star Wars* movies on video and we watched them." I'm like, "I know, I know. I was there," and I carry on hugging the goy for ages, until I've lost all track of time.

Me and Oisínn, roysh, we're bored off our faces in the bor, so we head over to the Orts block, to try to catch Fionn coming out of psychology, but he's still in the lecture hall so we head in, roysh, and sit down the back and oh my God I have never seen so many amazing-looking birds in my life. Fionn told me before that, like, all the bimbos who do Orts always choose either philosophy or psychology because, what was it, they think they pass for, like, depth? I don't know about that, roysh, but I turn around to Oisínn to tell him that if I could have a fourth shot at the Leaving, maybe aim for points this time rather than just trying to pass the thing, I'd try to end up in here. I go to tell him this, roysh, but he's already talking to this bird beside him, Elinor I think her name is, I know her to see from Clone 92, looks a little bit like Maria Grazia Cucinotta, and she's asking Oisínn has he heard that Kelly is thinking of going to Australia for the year, and I wonder whether she's talking about Kelly who was in the Institute with us last year, tall girl, amazing bod, always has, like, sunglasses in her hair. I still can't see Fionn. Up the front, roysh, we hear all this, like, sniggering and there's these four Nure goys we know – they're sound, even though they're Gick, like – and they're sitting behind this bird in a pink Hobo top, roysh, and they've slipped something into her hood, a photograph or something. Of course we find out later, roysh, that the goys had gone on a real knacker's holiday, we're talking Playa del Ingles or something, after they'd finished the Leaving, roysh, and the picture was of Kenno's dick, which the rest of the goys took when he was locked. So this ends up in your one's hood, roysh, and of course she's the last one in the whole focking lecture hall to cop it, but when she finally realises there's something going on, she reaches back, pulls the picture out, jumps up, goes, "Oh my God, Oh my God, Oh my God", and runs out of the place. Seriously funny.

I'm on the Leopardstown Road, roysh, and this woman's, like, trying to get out onto the road, but I'm just, like, refusing to let her out, because I never give way to women, it's a rule I have, because they never EVER give way on the road, they never do, and even if you do give way to them, let them out of, like, a petrol station or a side street or some shit, they never give you a wave to say thank-you, roysh, or they never flash their hazard lights, it's like it's expected of you. So this one, roysh, she's focking raging and she beeps me, so I just turn around, give her a big smile and then the finger, and then a goy in a Golf GTI, like the one I'm getting for Christmas except in blue, he comes up behind me and he's not going to let her out either, and she is going spare. We're talking total here as well. But then, roysh, I get up to the roundabout at the top of the road and I'm, like, waiting for, like, ten minutes or something and there's still no break in the focking cars. And Westlife are on the radio, flying without focking wings, and I flick over but it's, like, Emma Bunton and Britney Spears and other shite, and Venetia Quick, who says there's an accident to watch ait for on the Meath Raid, and raidworks on Saith King Street are causing major delays around Stephen's Green, and diversions are in operation on the Saith Circular Raid between Donore Avenue and Kelly's Corner due to ESB works in operation. And if there's not a break in the cors soon, I'm going to focking...

JP sends me a text message, roysh, and it's like, "SCORED A JUDGE'S DAUGHTER LAST NIGHT. AFFLUENCE."

It's the day before Christmas Eve, roysh, and we're all having drinks in The Bailey, middle of the afternoon, and Sorcha hands Aoife a present, roysh, and Aoife goes, "Oh my God, I haven't got yours with me. I was going to wait until tomorrow night." Sorcha says it doesn't matter and Aoife opens the present and it's, like, a *Friends* video. Aoife's face lights up and Sorcha goes, "I hope you haven't already got that one", and then Aoife's face drops, roysh, and she's like, "Oh shit, I have." Sorcha's like, "I don't believe it. I phoned up your mum and asked her to check whether you had Series 5, Episodes 17-20, the one where Rachel smokes, and she said you didn't." Aoife's like, "She is SUCH a stupid bitch, my mother. It's Series 3, Episodes 17-20 that I don't have." Emer, who's, like, first year Marketing, Advertising and Public Relations in LSB, she goes, "Which one is that?" and Aoife's there, "The one with the Princess Leia fantasy." Emer says that is SUCH a good episode and Sorcha says it's alright because she kept the receipt just in case.

Emer says there were three refugees outside her old dear's shop all day yesterday, wrecking everyone's head with their music, those bloody accordions, and Erika says she read somewhere that they're making up to a thousand pounds a day from begging and busking and Emer goes, "If you could call it busking." I don't know why, roysh, but I turn around and go, "Why don't you lay off the Romanians?" and everyone at the table turns to me, roysh, and looks at me like I'm totally off my head and I probably am because I cannot believe I said it myself. Erika goes, "Sorry, Ross, where is this coming from?" I'm like, "I don't know. I mean, it's Christmas. Could we not be, like, a bit more, I don't know... caring?" Emer goes, "Caring? Caring? HELLO? This is Ross O'Carroll-Kelly I'm talking to, isn't it? Most selfish bastard who ever lived?" I'm like, "I'm not selfish." And Aoife goes, "Ross, Bronwen told us all about you. You remember Bronwen? You were with her at the Loreto Dalkey pre-debs?" I'm like, "I know who she is." And Aoife goes, "Well according to her, you bought a packet of condoms, ribbed, extra-sensitive, for her pleasure. And you tried to put one on inside out." I'm there, "That was a focking accident and she knows it", but everyone's cracking their shites laughing and I go, "Look, all I'm saying is, you know, these refugees, they've lost, like, their homes and shit. I mean, how would you like it if you were suddenly dropped in the middle of, I don't know... Budapest." Erika goes, "The capital of Romania, Ross, is Bucharest. And they have Prada there. And Amanda Wakeley."

Christmas in my gaff is a complete mare and we're talking complete here. I wake up in the morning, roysh, about eleven o'clock, feeling pretty shabby I have to say, a feed of pints the night before, I'm hanging big-style and I can hear the old pair downstairs all focking over each other. We're talking total borf-fest here. It's all, like, squealing and "Ooo, it's just what I wanted", roysh, and I go downstairs to tell the two of them to keep it down. Turns out, roysh, the old dear bought the old man a Callaway ERC2 driver and he bought her, like, jewellery, a shitload of Lladro and a midweek break at the Powerscourt Springs and they're, like, hugging and kissing each other, roysh, and it's all 'Happy Christmas, Darling', and I'm finding it pretty hord to keep my toast down.

They've got me a Golf GTI, roysh, black, total babe magnet, or should I say they're going to get me one. I told them to wait until the new year, roysh, to, like, get the 01D reg. So anyway, roysh, the old dear hands me this present and she's like, "Oh, we wanted you to have something to open on the day", and I'm like, "Yeah, roysh. What am I supposed to say, yippee-hoo?" but I open it, roysh, just to keep them happy and it's a Motorola T2288, we're talking a crappy eleven ringtones, we're talking no vibration alert, we are talking only 210 minutes of battery talktime. I'm like, "Sorry, what is THIS supposed to be?" and the old man goes, "It's a mobile phone, Ross", and I'm like, "You are taking the total piss here. It's not even focking WAP-enabled", and I fock it across the table and go upstairs to, like, get dressed and shit. As I'm going up the stairs, I can hear the old dear asking the old man what WAP-enabled means, roysh, and then she says she's ruined Christmas and storts, like, bawling her eyes out, the attention-seeking bitch.

About, like, ten minutes, roysh, the old man shouts up the stairs to me and he's like, "Don't be too long, Ross. We're going to go to twelve mass. As a family", and I'm like, "Get real, will you? You retord", but I end up going anyway, roysh, anything for an easy life, and it's the usual crack, Holy Mary mother of God blah blah blah, and I end up sitting there for the whole of mass, texting Christian, Fionn and everyone else I know to give them, like, my new number and tell them I might see them L8ER.

Eabha, roysh, this friend of Sorcha, my ex who's, like, doing the DBS in Carysfort, she actually phones me back straight away to say thanks for the Burberry scorf, which I bought her pretty much to piss off Sorcha, who was basically dropping hints to me that she wanted one herself. So anyway, Eabha rings, roysh, and I have totally forgotten that the ringtone is switched to, like, Auld Lang Syne, and when it goes off this woman sitting in front of me, roysh, she turns around and gives me a total filthy and I'm there, "Hang on a sec, Eabha", and I'm like, "Turn the fock around", and your one does. And oh my God, roysh, you should have SEEN the state of my old dear. We're talking dressed to focking kill here. And it's, like, guess who spent a grand in Pia Bang yesterday. When she comes back from communion, roysh, I hear her turn to the old man and go, "That's the same coat that Ann Marie was wearing last year", and the old man goes, "Oh my God", out of the corner of his mouth.

Dinner is painful. Dermot and Anita, these, like, friends of the old pair, roysh, they're invited around and of course the whole conversation is dominated by this new campaign they're storted, which is, like, Move Funderland to the Northside. I mean, we don't live anywhere near the focking RDS, roysh, but Anita lives on Sandymount Avenue and of course the old dear can't resist it, keeps saying that Anita was SO helpful with the Foxrock Against Total Skangers anti-halting site campaign, roysh, that she simply HAD to get involved. She's a complete spa. She's there going, "I don't know how you cope, Anita, I really don't." And Anita's there going, "We've put up with it for twenty years, Fionnuala. Gangs of what can only be described as gurriers walking by, carrying giant elephants, urinating in our gardens, off to get the Dort to what's this it's called, Kilbarrack, and God knows wherever else." She's talking, roysh, with her mouth full, we're talking turkey and stuffing and roast potatoes, and I actually feel like saying something to the bitch, but I don't think anyone would even hear me if I did. She's going, "Now don't get me wrong, Charles. We're not anti Funderland, are we Dermot? But somewhere like, I don't know, Bally-mun, would be a more appropriate place for it, surely."

The old dear's like, "Don't get upset, Anita. Charles will print out those posters for you tomorrow. Have another drink." And Anita, roysh, you can see she's storting to get emotional, already half pissed on Baileys and mulled wine, and she's going, "I'm going to picket the RDS, Fionnuala. On my own if I have to. But I'm going to do it. I will." This goes on for ages and I basically can't take it anymore, roysh, and I end up going, "Is this a family dinner or a focking campaign meeting?" And everything goes silent. The old man goes, "Well, what would you like to talk about, Ross?" and I sort of, like, don't know what to say, roysh, so I just end up telling them what a bunch of retords they look in their paper hats and the old man goes, "Ross, if you can't keep a civil tongue in your head, I suggest you leave the table", and I'm like, "With focking pleasure", and I grab three cans out the fridge and head into the sitting-room to watch the Bond movie.

So I'm sitting there, roysh, and it's, like, *Octopussy*, and I'm knocking back the beers, milling into the old Quality Street, and my phone rings and it's, like, Fionn and I'm just like, "Yoh Fionn, happy Christmas my man, speak to me." He goes, "Hey, Ross. Greetings and felicitations to you and yours." I'm there, "What time did you leave the M1 last night?" He goes, "Fock knows, it was late. Hey, you will not BELIEVE who I was with last night." I'm like, "Who?" and he goes, "Esme." I'm like, "Who's Esme?" even though I know damn well who she is, roysh, and he goes, "Esme. HELLO? Second year business in Portobello? Looks like Elize Dushku. Or so you said." I tried to be with her two weeks ago in Anabel's and completely crashed and burned. I'm there, "I never said she looked like Elize Dushku." Fionn goes, "Hey, I know you tried to get in there, Ross. No hard feelings, man. It turns out she's mad into goys with blond hair." I'm like, "And glasses?" He goes, "She focking loves glasses, Ross. Thinks they're a sign of intelligence." I'm there, "What an airhead." He goes, "I'm not after her mind, Ross." I'm there, "I never said she looks like Elize Dushku" and he's like, "Anyone with any information on the whereabouts of Ross O'Carroll-Kelly's dignity, would they please contact Gardaí at Cabinteely?"

I decide to change the subject. I'm like, "Did Christian end up with that bird he was talking to? What's her name, Nicki?" Fionn goes, "Young Obi Wan, no, he ended up with this total focking stunner. She's from Iceland." I'm like, "You mean the country?" He goes, "No, the focking supermarket. Of course the country, Ross. Get with the programme, will you?" I'm like, "Sorry, man. Distracted. The olds are wrecking my head, as per usual." He goes, "Mare." I'm like, "The old man is even talking about inviting Gerry Thornley over for New Year. He goes, "Whoa, heavy shit, dude. Are they bosom buddies now or something?" I'm like, "Do not go there, my man. Do not go there."

He's like, "Hey, I saw Sorcha at mass this morning. She is not a happy camper." I'm like, "Is she pissed off with me?" He goes, "Seems to be. I asked her whether she'd been talking to you and she went ballistic. We're talking totally here." I'm like, "Starring role in a period costume drama, maybe?" He goes, "That's what I thought. Then I wondered whether she'd found out about you and Erika." I'm like, "There's no chance of that." He goes, "What's the story with you two?" I'm there, "No story, Fionn. I was with her and..." He's like, "And nothing, Ross. Look, take my advice..." I'm like, "I don't need your advice." He goes, "TAKE my advice, Ross, I know what I'm talking about. Do NOT go there." I'm like, "JP reckons she's saving herself for Ben Affleck." He goes, "It's not that, Ross. She's into horses." I'm like, "What the fock does that have to do with anything?" He goes, "Take it from someone who's pissing his way through first year psychology. I know what I'm talking about. Girls who are into horses are just... different. No girl who's into horses can ever truly love a goy." I'm there, "Is that because of the size of their..." and he's, "Focking hell, Ross, here I am trying to share with you the wealth of my experience in studying the workings of the female mind and all you can think of is your focking shlong." Fionn's theories are, like, such bullshit, roysh, but I'm curious at this stage, so I ask him what he's going on about. He's there, "Think about all the girls we know who have horses. We're talking Alyson Berry. Amy Holden. Caoimhe Kelly. We're talking Ruth Richards. What have they all got in common?" I'm like, "I've been with them all." He goes, "That goes without saying, Ross. But what else?" I'm like, "They've all got horses." He goes, "And?" I'm like, "I don't know." He's there, "They're all stuck-up bitches, aren't they? Stuck-up, stubborn, cold, moody, selfish. All qualities you associate with horses." I'm like, "Bullshit." He goes, "Horses aren't nice animals, Ross. They're not loyal. They're not friendly. And they certainly don't need human love. All they want off us is food and if you don't have focking carrots and apples and, I don't know, hay for them to eat every day, they go into a sulk."

I'm there, "Where is this going, Fionn?" He goes, "Girls like Erika, Ross, they've been trying their whole lives to relate to these animals but they can't. Erika knows that however much she feeds her horse, brushes him, cleans him, the animal is never going to feel the same way about her as she does about it. The first love of her life was unrequited, you could say. And that's fucked her up. And then it's a life-long battle to try to win over the horse, make it love her back. And the more time you spend with an animal like that the more you become like it, we're talking cold and moody and selfish, basically stuck-up. And any girl whose father buys her a horse when she's eight, well she's not exactly getting the best start in life, is she?" I'm there, "Alright, alright. Listen, I've got to go. I'll call you later."

When I get off the phone, roysh, I'm in a bit of a fouler, and the next thing I hear is, like, the old dear coming into the room, pissed on mulled wine and she has this big, like, heart-shaped box of Butler's chocolates under her arm. I'm there, "What do you want?" She goes, "Three o'clock, Ross. The Queen's speech" and I'm like, "If you think you're coming in here to watch that bullshit, you can think again." She goes, "It's only ten minutes long" and I'm there, "HELLO? There are six other televisions in this house. Watch one of them." And she focks off.

I sit around for another, like, ten or fifteen minutes, roysh, thinking about whether I should ring Erika. The best way to play it, I decide, is, Kool and the Gang, so I phone her up, roysh, and I'm like, "Hey babe, how the hell are you?" She goes, "Who is this?" sounding like she's pretty pissed off about something. I'm like, "It's Ross. Just wondering how your Christmas was going?" She goes, "Look, I'm going to save you a lot of heartache, Ross, and save myself a major headache by telling you again that I HAVE NO INTEREST IN YOU." I'm there, "Hey, why so hostile, babe?" She goes, "I'm only stretching this conversation beyond one sentence because I want you to get it into your head, Ross. I'm not interested." I'm there, "Well, you seemed pretty interested a couple of weeks ago, up at the stables..." She goes, "Grow up, will you? If you must know, I did that because I was pissed off with Sorcha." I'm like, "Sorcha?" She's there, "Yes. You know, your girlfriend. *All this subtext is making me tired.*" I have to say, she does Sorcha's voice really well. I'm like, "So it meant nothing to you?" She goes, "It's use and abuse, Ross. That's the name of the game. You of all people should know that."

I'm like, "Look why don't I call over to your gaff?" She storts, like, laughing, roysh, and she goes, "You really think that under this hard outer shell there's a little girl who's going to melt in your arms when she hears all your bullshit lines, don't you?" I'm like, "You did in the past." She goes, "Ross, we were at school then. I was 16. And that was back in the days when you were someone." I'm like, "What do you mean when I was someone?" She goes, "You were on the senior rugby team, Ross. Being with you was, like, a status thing. I mean, who are you now? You're doing sports management for fock's sake. You're not even playing for UCD." I'm like, "Yeah, I've been mostly chilling this year. I mean, I so have to get my finger out, I know that." She just laughs. I go, "The goy who has my place on the team, Jamie Thompson, he's crap. He's a focking Michael's boy, for fock's sake. I could easily take his place. If I do, would you be interested then?"

She tells me I'm making a fool of myself, roysh, then says she has neither the energy nor the interest to continue the conversation further and she hangs up. I think about calling her back, roysh, but she's left me, like, totally shell-shocked. My name used to mean something. Every girl wanted to say she'd been with Ross O'Carroll-Kelly. Time has moved on, I guess.

I go to the old man's study and grab the tape of the senior cup final, roysh, and I fast-forward it to my winning try and spend the next, like, twenty minutes watching it and then rewinding it and watching it over and over again, while in the kitchen the old dear puts on her focking Charlotte Church album and the old man gives one of his big false laughs to some obviously unfunny thing that, like, Dermot has said? Rewind and play. Rewind and play. Then my interview with Ryle Nugent. "That's a good question, Ryle. I can't take all the credit for this victory, though. A lot of it has to go to the goys." And in the background, roysh, you can see all these blue jumpers. Mounties. We're talking hundreds of them. And I think I can even make out Erika – her hair was shorter then – hanging on every word. I think I might have even been with her that night. I put the lid back on the Quality Street, knock back the last of the cans and make my New Year's resolutions. Get fit. Get on the UCD team. Get Erika. Then I go into the kitchen and tell the old man to keep the focking fake laughter down.

I call out to Sorcha's gaff on Stephen's Day, roysh, and it's the usual crack from her old dear, who SO wants me to get back with her daughter it's not funny, and she's all over me, we're talking all over here, it's all hugs and kisses and I'm just there going. 'Guess who got a bottle of Chanel No 5 for Christmas'. The gaff is full, of course. The Lalors always have, like, half the focking world around to eat the Christmas leftovers and, when the old dear's finished air-kissing and squeezing the shit out of me, she leads me around the house, introducing me to aunts and uncles and neighbours and clients of the old man. Sometimes she goes, "This is Ross O'Carroll-Kelly, Sorcha's friend. He was on the Castlerock team that won the cup" and other times it's, "This is Ross, Charles O'Carroll-Kelly's son, very good friends with Sorcha". Then she offers me, in the following order, a slice of banoffi, a glass of mulled wine, a turkey and stuffing toasted sandwich, a piece of plum-pudding, a can of lager, and I say no to all of them and then there's pretty much nothing else to say, roysh, and we're both standing there like a couple of spare pricks, so she just tells me that Sorcha's in her room and to go on up to her.

She's lying on her bed, roysh, wearing her black Armani jeans and a white Lacoste airtex with the collar up, and she's, like, flicking through the channels on the telly. She doesn't acknowledge me and I just sort of, like, hang around in the doorway and I ask her whether she's still pissed off with me and she goes, "Why would I be pissed off with you, Ross?" Her room has actually been decorated, pretty recently I'd say, and I tell her that it's changed a good bit and she looks at me for the first time and goes, "It has changed, Ross. The last time you were in here you were with my little sister", and I turn around and stort, like, heading downstairs, but she calls me back and says she's sorry and, like, gives me a hug and wishes me a merry Christmas. She goes, "I don't know why I insist on reliving in excruciating detail one of the most painful experiences of our lives. Maybe it's my perversely self-deprecating way of moving on. Or maybe I'm still trying to punish you."

I sit down on the bed and she lies down with her head on my lap and asks me to, like, pet her face, which is something I used to always do when we were, like, going out together, and I can't work out whether she actually wants to be with me or whether it's just, like, a prick tease, but I do it anyway. I ask her why she's not downstairs at the porty and she goes, "Because basically I'm tired of my mother's projection fantasies", and I don't have a focking clue what she's talking about, roysh, so I just go, "Bummer." Then she says that the Millennium has turned out to be one complete bummer and that Killian was the only decent thing that happened to her in the year 2000. I'm like, "Is this the 28-year-old?" and she nods and goes, "I should say that Killian and you were the only good decent things that happened this year", and all of a sudden, roysh, I'm pretty certain that I'm going to end up, like, getting my bit here and I stop petting her face and go, "What do you mean I was one of the decent things that happened?" and she goes, "Well, not so much you, Ross, as us. After years of gratuitous self-examination, we've finally got past that whole relationship checkmate thing."

Again, I haven't a focking clue what she's saying, roysh, but I get the impression that she's trying to get across the point that she's not actually interested in me anymore, which is complete bullshit I know, because I notice she has *The Very Best of Ennio Morricone*, the CD I bought her for her birthday last year, on her bedside locker and I'm pretty sure that before I arrived she was listening to, I think it's called 'Gabriel's Oboe', wondering whether I was going to call up. But she's obviously playing hard to get, roysh, so I sort of, like, change tack and go, "How's Erika?" and suddenly she's like, "Fine. Why?" I'm like, "No reason. Just asking." And Sorcha sits up and goes, "What's all this sudden interest you have in Erika? Do you want to be with her, is that it?" I didn't expect her to be so, like, direct, roysh, and I'm like, "Spare me", but it's not very convincing, roysh, and I can feel myself going a bit red. She goes, "Anyway, Ross, nothing that girl does would bother me anymore." And I'm like, "Are you two not talking again?" and she's there, "She said in the pub the other night that wheelie bins are working class. Can you believe that?"

We lie there on the bed for, like, an hour. *The Royle Family* comes on and Sorcha says she wishes her family could be more like them. Eventually, roysh, I tell her I've got to go and she tells me she's really happy I called up, that Christmas wouldn't be the same without seeing me and that she's glad we're over "that whole relationship trauma". She takes off her scrunchy, roysh, slips it onto her wrist, shakes her hair free and then smoothes it back into a low ponytail again, puts it back in the scrunchy and then pulls five or six, like, strands of hair loose again.

As I'm leaving, roysh, I tell her I want to ask her something, like, awkward and she goes, "What is it, Ross?" and I'm like, "I'm worried about Christian." She goes, "Every time I see him lately he's locked, Ross" and I'm there, "I know you won't tell anyone this, Sorcha, but his parents are splitting up." She goes, "Trevor and Andrea? Oh my God that is SUCH a shock." I'm there, "Christian's not, I don't know, coping very well. He's, like, totally messed up about it. And I don't know what to say to him to, like, make it better I suppose." Sorcha gives me a hug and tells me just to be myself and to be there for him. She goes, "Just be yourself and be there for him."

# Chapter Three

The one where Ross
turns to the Dark Side

I'm in Stillorgan Shopping Centre, roysh, doing a bit of shopping, actually looking for a new pair of rugby boots, and I'm backing out of a porking space when the phone rings and it's, like, Keevo. He's like, "Ross, I've a good one for you." I'm there, "Keevo, now is not a good time, my man." He's like, "It won't take long." I'm like, "What is it?" He goes, "Think of a number between one and ten." And I'm like, "Okay, hang on... Right, got one." He goes, "Roysh, add four." I'm like, "Okay." He goes, "Now, double it." And I'm like, "Hold on, hold on... Right." He's there, "Now, halve it." And I'm like, "Yeah." Then he goes, "Take away four." I'm like, "Yyyeah?" And he goes, "And you're left with six." I'm like, "No. I'm left with four." He goes, "Oh, roysh. No, it doesn't always work."

And he hangs up. And this SO worries me, roysh, because Keevo is, like, second year theoretical physics.

When we were in, like, first year in school, roysh, Christian's mum and dad split up for, like, six months or something and though Christian never really spoke about it, pretty much everyone knew that it was because his old man was basically having an affair with this other woman who was, like, a partner in the same company as him. His old man's, like, a barrister. Anyway, roysh, while all this shit was going down, Christian was sent to Castlerock to board and his sister, roysh, Iseult, she boarded at Alexandra, just for, like, the

46

year, just while the old pair were working things out.

Christian said it was, like, the most amazing year of his life, but I knew he hated it a couple of the goys I knew from the junior cup team said he used to cry pretty much every night when the lights were off and he thought no-one could, like, hear him and shit?

I used to stay back after school for a couple of hours, roysh, supposedly to do supervised study, that's what I told my old pair, but we'd basically just hang out, mostly chatting about rugby and birds we wanted to snog, and never about his old pair. And even though, roysh, technically I shouldn't have been still in the school grounds at, like, half-seven at night, the priests never said anything to me, roysh, because, well basically I think it was because they knew the shit that Christian was going through and having his best mate there just, like, made it better for him.

I hated going home, because it was like he was in prison and I was just, like, visiting him, and every night, roysh, when it was time for me to head, he'd ask me to stay a bit longer and when I'd tell him that I had to get my bus, he'd say that there's a 46a every, like, ten minutes.

It seems so long ago now. I remember this one time, roysh, and this is going to sound totally weird, but we were hanging out at the rugby pitch next to the dorms, basically lying on the grass, watching it get dark, talking about girls, mostly Karyn Flynn and Jessica Kennedy, these two Mounties we were into. This thing, roysh, had been on my mind for about a week, so I turns around to him and I'm like, "Christian, can I ask you something?" and he goes, "What?" and I'm there, "You know that thing they say about magpies? That it's, like, one for sorrow, two for joy, three for a girl..." I can see him now, roysh, all of a sudden sitting up, so he's, like, leaning on his elbows. He went, "What about it?" And I went, "I saw four the other day. Does that mean I'm..." He broke his shite laughing and he went, "You are so weird, Ross", and then he broke his shite laughing again.

Sophie, roysh, she takes, like, five minutes to chew one mouthful of pop-corn, roysh, and it is seriously wrecking my head and when I ask her what the fock she's doing, roysh, she says she read in some magazine, maybe *Cosmo* or *InStyle*, that you don't put on as much weight if you, like, chew your food for longer, but watching her is pissing me off. Chloë, who's, like, second year International Commerce with German, SO like Heidi Klum it's unbelievable, I scored her at the Traffic Light Ball, roysh, she asks Sophie whether she's seen Valerie lately and Sophie goes, "Valerie as in first year strategic marketing in LSB?" and Chloë nods and says she has put on SO much weight and she's not being a bitch or anything but OH MY GOD she's actually a size sixteen and Sophie asks her how she knows and Chloë tells her that she's storted working in Benetton, just to get money together for Australia if she decides to go for the year, and Valerie came into the shop last week. Sophie goes, "Oh my God she used to be SO gorgeous. She brought Alex Gaffney to the Holy Child Killiney debs." And Chloë goes, "I know".

I knock back the rest of my Coke, roysh, and I get up to go and Sophie asks me whether I've got a lecture this afternoon. I'm like, "I had a ten o'clock but I skipped it. I'm just going off to practice my kicking for a couple of hours." She asks me whether I've been talking to Sorcha. I say no, roysh, so she tells me the plan for Saturday night has changed, that Gisele has decided not to have her going-away somewhere in town, because the problem with Clone 92 is that if the bouncers, like, turn you away, then that's your night over, you're stranded in Leopardstown. She says that Erika won't go there anyway, because she reckons it's full of skobies.

I bump into the goys at the blob, we're talking Christian and Oisínn, and they're about to go on the serious lash with Fionn. Oisínn goes, "Where are you going?" I'm like, "Training." Oisínn's like, "Training? For what?" I'm like, "Rugby. HELLO? We are all doing SPORTS scholarships, remember?" And Christian's there, "Is this because of what it says on the door of the jacks." Oisínn's there, "Leave it, Christian" and I'm like, "What does it say in the jacks?" Oisínn goes, "You don't want to know. Just something about you being finished. Past it. You have had a lot of injuries, Ross." Christian goes, "They call you Tampax, Ross. One week in and then three weeks out." I'm like, "They call me that?" and Oisínn goes, "Some do. You'd very bad luck with injuries, though."

So I head down to the gym, roysh, do some stretches and shit, and then do half an hour on the treadmill, after which I'm, like, totally shagged. But I am SO determined to get fit, roysh, that I go right through the pain barrier. I do, like, half-and-hour on the bike and a few weights and then I head out with a ball to, like, practice my kicking. When I get to the field, roysh, who's there before me only Jamie Thompson, the knob whose place on the team I'm about to take. He's, like, practicing his kicking as well, roysh, and when he sees me he storts totally gicking himself. I stand there and watch him for, like, twenty minutes, really psyching the goy out of it and in the end I'm not being a bastard or anything but the goy couldn't hit a donkey's orse with a banjo. He's taking kicks from, like, different angles, roysh, and even in front of the post he goes and misses and he's getting, like, totally flustered, doesn't have the big-match temperament, as Sooty, our old coach, used to say. It's no wonder UCD are focked.

When he finally gets one between the posts, roysh, I just stort clapping, sort of, like, sarcastically. Then I head over and stand in front of him and I've got my old Castlerock jersey on, roysh, and I point to the badge and go, "You know what this means, don't you?" He goes, "It means you went to a school for wankers". I'm like, "It actually means that you can go home now" and then I go, "You're excess baggage", which I have to say I'm pretty pleased with, roysh, even though I don't know where I got it from. He goes, "You're living on past glories", so I push him out of the way and I'm just there, "Learn from the master." I put the ball down, roysh, and stort kicking at the goal he's been using and he stands there and watches me putting it straight between the posts from, like, every angle you can think of. I'm focking on fire. Doesn't matter what I do, I can't miss. He watches me for, like, ten or fifteen minutes and then I decide I've punished him enough and, as I'm leaving, I turn to him and go, "Thanks for keeping my place warm."

I have my shower and get changed and it's, like, only three o'clock, so I phone Christian on his mobile, roysh, and he tells me they all ended up heading into town and they're in the Bailey, so I drive in, pork the cor on Stephen's Green and head down. I am in SUCH good form. I'm like, "I'm back, goys. I am SO back." Oisínn goes, "Pint?" I'm like, "Orange juice." And Fionn makes this, like, wolf-whistling sound and then high-fives me. Christian, who's already totally shit-faced, he grabs me around the neck and goes, "Remember, if you choose the quick and easy path as Vader did, you will become an agent of evil. You must complete your training." I'm like, "My training is complete, Obi Wan", sort of, like, playing along. "I'm going to kick orse".

I have a couple of glasses of orange juice, but the goys are on a totally different buzz to me, so I end up heading off after a couple of hours and I'm in such a good mood I even think about phoning Erika on the way back to the cor, but it's, like, early days yet and in the end I don't bother. My car – we're talking my new Golf GTI here – has been clamped. I'm just there going, that is SO not on. I get onto the old man, roysh, and I'm there, "I need your credit cord number." He goes, "What for?" I'm like, "No time to go into all that. Just gimme the number." The dickhead, roysh, he's there, "It's a bit of an awkward time, Ross. I'm in a meeting." I'm like, "Well just give me the focking number then and stop blabbing on", which he eventually does. I phone up the number on the notice that's stuck to my windscreen and I go, "Yeah, you've put a clamp on my cor. Take it off. Here's my credit cord number. You've got fifteen minutes." He takes down the number, roysh, and I go, "And make sure you get all the glue off my windscreen or I'll sue your focking orses." He goes, "Can I just take your name, sir?" I'm like, "It's Ross O'Carroll Kelly. And if you haven't heard it before, don't worry. You will."

I get this letter from the bank, roysh, saying I've been approved for a £10,000 personal loan, which is, like, weird, because I never focking applied for one.

Aoife says that Graham, some dickhead she knows from Anabel's, is SO good-looking that every girl in her year wants to be with him but Sorcha says he is SUCH a Chandler when it comes to commitment and I am already beginning to regret meeting the girls for lunch and my eyes, roysh, they keep, like, wandering over to where Erika is sitting with this really bored expression on her face, like she's pissed off with everyone at the table. I get out my phone, roysh, and text her and it's, like, "WAN 2 TLK?" and a couple of seconds later her phone beeps and she, like, reads the message and tells me in front of, like, everyone that I'm a sad bastard. I can feel Sorcha staring at me, roysh, so I try to change the subject by asking Aoife how her brother's getting on with Clontorf, but before she can answer, roysh, this waitress comes over and tells Emer that people aren't allowed to eat their own, like, food on the premises. And Emer just goes, "HELLO? It's only a bag of popcorn?" and the waitress is like, "It doesn't matter. House rules" and Emer puts the bag away really slowly, roysh, while giving the waitress a total filthy and the waitress goes again, "I'm sorry, it's house rules", but Emer doesn't answer, just carries on staring her out of it.

The conversation suddenly moves onto some bird called Alison, who's, like, second year tourism in LSB and is SO thin, according to Emer, and Aoife goes OH MY GOD did you see the dress she wore to Melissa Berry's 21st and Sorcha asks her what it was like and Aoife says it was a Chanel. Emer says that Alison is thinking of going to Australia for the year and so, apparently, are Caoimhe Kelly, who I'm pretty sure I was with at the Traffic Light Ball, and Elaine Anders, who I've never focking heard of. Aoife tells Sorcha she should go to Australia for the year herself and Sorcha tells Aoife she SO should go as well. Emer was in Lillies on Saturday night but there was, like, no-one really in there, unless of course you call Amanda Byram and the lead singer from OTT someone, which she doesn't.

Sorcha goes, "Oh my God I forgot to tell you, Claire is thinking of entering the Bray Festival Queen competition" and Erika all of a sudden looks up and goes, "Oh your little friend, the one who thinks coleslaw is cosmopolitan? Yes, that would be so her alright" and she gets up, roysh, picks up her bags, we're talking Carl Scarpa, Morgan and Blue Eriu, and just, like, walks out of the place, leaving her lunch on the table, and her Marlboro Lights. Aoife says that girl has SUCH an attitude problem and Sorcha tells her not to worry, she's sure Ross won't mind paying for her Caesar wrap, which to be honest I've no problem with. And Emer says the new series of Ally McBeal is SO not as good as the last one.

The traffic on the Stillorgan dual-carriageway is a mare and we are talking total here. I open the glove compartment, roysh, to get my Eminem CD and it's, like, gone. So I phones the house, roysh, and the old man picks up the phone and he can tell I'm seriously pissed off and he goes, "I take it you've read it then?" I'm like, "What are you talking about?" He goes, "And to think I almost invited that man over here for New Year. I suppose he's never been a friend of schools rugby. We knew that." I go, "I don't even want to know what you are bullshitting on about. Just put the old dear on." So he gets her, roysh, and I'm like, "Answer me one question and do NOT yank my chain on this one. What have you done with my Eminem CD?" She goes, "I took it back to the shop, Ross. Disgusting, some of the things he was singing about. It was eff this and you're an effing that, mother this and mother the other." I'm like, "It's none of your focking business what I listen to." She goes, "You left it in the CD player in the kitchen, Ross. I thought it was my Celine Dion album. Delma was here for coffee." And she's like, "I'm not the only one who brought it back, by the way. The young lady in the shop told me it's the most returned record they've ever sold. I'd be worried about the influence that that kind of thing might have on you, Ross." I'm like, "Bitch, I'm a kill you", and I hang up, roysh, and punch the FOCKING dashboard and and and FOCK.

And to cap it all the traffic is actually getting focking worse and how many focking gears does that car in front of me have. I turn on the radio, roysh, but I can't get a decent song, it's all Christina Aguilera and Ronan focking Keating and I'm flipping from channel to channel but it's like, "normal lending criteria and terms and conditions apply", and "regular savings and higher returns with personal investment plans", and "help bridge the recruitment gap by skilling up your existing workforce". And the slip light is out of action on the main streesh in Bray and there's bad flooding around Baker's Coyner and electrical cables are dain on the Belgord Raid and there's the usual delays on all routes out of the city, including the Naas Raid, the Navan Raid and the South Circular Raid...

I bump into Erika in Finnegan's Break and she's, like, sipping a glass of boiling water, roysh, I ask her what she's doing for the afternoon and she says she's going to the orthodontist. I'm like, "Have you heard I'm back playing rugby?" and she stubs out a Marlboro Light and goes, "This affects me how?" I ask her what time she's be finished at the dentist and she says it's the orthodontist and I'm like, "Same thing", and she just looks me up and down and goes, "Hordly."

A few months ago, roysh, before I decided to lay off the sauce and go back training, me and the goys – we're talking Christian, Fionn, Oisínn, Gavin, all those – we were out on the lash, roysh, a Monday night in Peg's, pound a pint, the usual crack and, like, when it was over we all headed back to Oisínn's gaff on Shrewsbury Road to get, like, food and a taxi and shit. So we were, like, in the kitchen, roysh, and I looked over at Oisínn – he's had, like, nine or ten pints at this stage – and the goy's eating a block of focking lard. We are talking LARD here. At first, roysh, I thought it was the usual crack, you know, absolutely storving but too shit-faced to cook, I mean the goy would eat focking anything, but then he tells us, roysh, that he's in training for, like, the Iron Stomach contest that the C&E society hold as part of rag week.

Turns out, roysh, that Oisínn decided to enter after he'd met a bunch of, like, Andrews dickheads in the Ass and Cart the previous weekend, all first year commerce heads who recognised him and storted giving him loads about what a shit school Castlerock was, roysh, brave men it has to be said because Oisínn is a focking huge bloke. But it was all like, "How many points did you get in the Leaving?" and "How many former Taoisigh went to your school?" and what with one thing and another this goy, Keyser, who Oisínn came pretty close to decking, he ended up, like, challenging him to see who had, like, the strongest stomach.

So rag week arrives, roysh, and we're all there in our Castlerock jerseys, giving it loads, and there's, like, seven or eight people in the competition, all sitting in a row, a few from Commerce, a couple from Science, but all eyes are on Oisínn and Keyser, who are the big-time favourites, and we're all there giving it, "You can't knock the Rock. You can't knock the Rock", totally intimidating the Andrews goys. So first, roysh, all the, like, contestants, are given a can of Holsten which is, like, six months past its sell-by date and, while they're drinking that, they have to eat a Weetabix with, like, soy sauce and lemon curd on it? One of them, roysh, we're talking one of the Science goys, he borfs straight away, so there's only, like, six of them left and we're all there giving it loads as they hand out the next thing they have to eat, which is, like, a pot of cold custard with, like, a spoonful of baked beans stirred into it, we're talking cold here, and a spoonful of treacle as well. Oh my God I thought I was going to, like, vom myself.

More Holsten. Then it's, like, a double shot of tequila, roysh, and then they all have to hit the deck and do, like, twenty sit-ups each. The next thing is a cold mince and onion pie with, like strawberry jam and Bonjela gum ointment on it and this girl sitting beside Oisínn, a real Commerce head, she just goes totally green, roysh, and we're talking totally here, and she borfs her ring up all over Oisínn, all over his chinos, all over his docksiders, all over everything. At this stage, I'm convinced that Oisínn is going to borf as well, but he manages to keep it in.

Then, roysh, we see one of the Andrews goys in the crowd, Henno, this total dickhead who's going out with Emma, not hockey Emma, we're talking Institute Emma, who I was sort of seeing when I was doing grinds. I look over at him, roysh, and give him the finger and he comes over and goes, "Your goy is going to lose". I'm there, "You seem pretty sure of yourself." And he goes, "There's something you don't know about Keyser. He has no taste buds, man. Lost them a couple of years ago in an unfortunate accident involving a flaming Sambucca. Tragic really. He can't taste any of that shit he's eating." I'm like, "Oh my God that is IT" and I storm up to the front and I tell Oisínn we're pulling him out of the competition. He's like, "No FOCKING way." When he says this, roysh, he has a mouthful of, like, beetroot and yoghurt, most of which ends up all over my jacket, we're talking my red Henri Lloyd sailing jacket here. I go, "Oisínn, Keyser's a freak. The goy has no taste buds." He thinks about this for, like, five seconds, roysh, swallowing what he has in his mouth, and goes, "So? Doesn't matter, Ross. We're Castlerock, remember? We never quit."

I have to say, roysh, I felt pretty emotional at that moment, but then I had to take a few steps backwards because everyone around me storted, like, spewing their guts up all over the place and suddenly there's only, like, Oisínn and Keyser left and it's, like, a two horse race. More Holsten. More tequila. A twenty-second squirt of, like, tomato sauce into each of their mouths. Oh my God how they didn't borf there and then I don't know. Another double shot of tequila. Hit the deck, twenty press-ups and then, like, twenty sit-ups. Then they've got to, like, put their heads back while one of the C&E goys comes up behind them and feeds them, like, a raw fish. Keyser is looking so cocky at this stage, roysh, dancing to the music and everything. A glass of cooking oil with a squirty cream head. Picked onions with ice cream. Mussels. A catfood sandwich with toothpaste and ketchup on it. Down they go.

Keyser looks like he could go on at this all day. Oisínn looks in trouble. He's knocking back the beers, though, probably to take the focking taste out of his mouth, and when he finishes another, it's like his eighth, he turns around to Keyser and goes, "Are you not drinking?" So Keyser, roysh, he's handed two cans by one of the C&E goys, who's noticed that he's only drunk, like, six, and Keyser decides he has to show off, he can't be seen to be drinking less than a Rock boy, so he shotguns the two cans and downs them. Next thing, roysh, you can actually see that the goy is going to borf, his face goes white and it's like he can't catch his breath, roysh, and he just leans over and spews his guts up all over the gaff. We all just, like, mobbed Oisínn, singing

Castlerock Uber Alles, the whole lot, then we're like, "SPEECH. SPEECH. SPEECH", and eventually, roysh, when he's, like, composed himself, Oisínn goes, "Thank you very much. I have to tell you that I knew all along about Keyser having no taste buds. It didn't bother me. For I also knew that Andrew's goys can't drink for shit. I believed that I could eat more than Keyser could drink. It was a gamble, but it worked." Christian turns to me, roysh, and goes, "That goy is a Jedi, Ross. A focking Jedi knight."

Oisínn heads off to Vincent's Hospital, roysh, and we head on in to town and tell him we'll meet him in the Temple later one. Ten o'clock, we're still all sitting around, waiting for the man of the moment to arrive and I think Fionn speaks for us all when he goes, "How long does it take to focking pump a goy out?" There's, like, loads of girls hanging around our table and shit and it's just like the night we won the cup, except they're actually wrecking our heads a bit because this should be, like, a night for the goys. The second Oisínn arrives, I think it's definitely going to be a case of ditch the bitches. The saps are actually, like, in competition with each other to see who's going to end up being with him when he arrives. Sarah Jane, who's, like, repeating first year law in Portobello, she goes, "My cousin actually knows Oisínn's sister really well." And the other bird, Bryana I think her name is, she goes, "HELLO? I was in Irish college with Blathnaid for two summers. She's one of my best friends." And Chloë, roysh, who's, like, second year International Commerce with French in UCD and really good friends with Sorcha, my ex, she asks me what Oisínn had to eat and I tell her, roysh, about the cold custard, the beans, the Weetabix and the raw fish, the mince and onion pies and the strawberry jam, and she goes, "Oh MY God, that is SO gross. Can you IMAGINE how many points that is?"

I have a copy of the *Pretty Woman* soundtrack in my cor, roysh, and I bring it everywhere I go. And we're talking everywhere. That song, 'Fallen', by Lauren Wood, roysh, birds love it. I've scored ten, maybe fifteen girls, to that song. They go mad for it.

It's the usual crack in college, doing fock-all, just basically chilling, taking it easy and shit. Hit the sports bor in the morning, read Wardy's report on the Clongowes match, played a few frames of Killer with, like, Oisínn and Christian, sent Rory down to 911 for the rolls, then headed to the computer room for the two hours of, like, free internet access. After that, roysh, the afternoon was pretty much our own, so me and the goys were, like, sitting around in Hilper's with Chloë, who's, like, first year B&L and Clodagh, who's repeating first year Orts and everyone has, like, their mobiles, their car keys and, in the girls' case, lip balm on the table, and Oisínn's talking about some goy in first year business who he says is a total faggot and all of a sudden, roysh, Chloë goes, "What have you got against gay people?" Oisínn's like, "Nothing" and Chloë goes, "You better not have, because I've got LOADS of friends who are gay." Clodagh says she has too but Chloë says she doesn't have as many as she has.

I have to say, roysh, that Chloë is a total honey, we're talking really well-stacked here, ex-Dalkey girl, SO like Emmanuelle Béart it's unbelievable, while Clodagh is a complete focking moon pig, though Christian said in Anabel's last Friday night, roysh, that he'd be prepared to, like, take a bullet for me if I'd any chance of being with Chloë. So we're sitting there, roysh, and Chloë is SO flirting her orse off with me it's unbelievable. She's there going, "Ross, would you be a complete dorling and go and get me a cup of boiling water." Of course, Fionn has to go and ruin it, roysh, going, "Why the fock do you girls drink that shit?" and Chloë's there, "Because it's good for your skin" and Clodagh goes, "And cold water, like, slows down your metabolism?" Chloë, who looks totally amazing in her light blue Ralph with the collar up and a baby blue sleeveless bubble jacket, goes, "Would you be a complete dorling, Ross, and get it for me? And a packet of Marlboro Lights as well" and I'm like, "Does the Pope shit in the woods?"

After lunch, there's, like, fock-all happening, so the five of us decide to head out to Stillorgan to, like, see a movie for the afternoon. Clodagh says she really wants to see *Cast Away*, roysh, and Chloë says that is SO a good idea. Clodagh says they actually filmed it in two sequences, roysh, and that Tom Hanks lost three stone in eight months to play the port of a goy who's, like, shipwrecked on a desert island. Fionn says that three stone in eight months is nothing, that anyone from the cast of *Friends* could do that in a long weekend, and even though I think it's, like, really funny, roysh, I notice that Chloë isn't laughing so I tell Fionn he's a knob and he goes, "Anyone with any information on the whereabouts of Ross's sense of humour, would they contact Gardaí at Stillorgan."

So we're about to head off, roysh, when all of a sudden this goy, Dowdy, who's, like, second year sports management, ex Clongowes boy and a total dickhead, he comes over and storts, like, chatting to the birds, asking them how they're fixed for the exams and shit. Clodagh says she hasn't done a tap all year and SO has to get her finger out of her orse it's not funny and then he turns around and asks us the same question, roysh, and we all, like, totally blank him. He's there, "Oh, I get it, the old school rivalry shit. All I'm saying, goys, is don't leave it too late to stort studying for the exams. I should know." I'm there, "HELLO? We're doing Sports Management." He goes, "I know. You've still got exams." I'm like, "I've been training my orse off for, like, two weeks now. I cannot BELIEVE they are pulling this shit on me now. How many exams are we talking? There's only, like, three subjects on the course. We can just get the notes off the internet, can't we?" He goes, "Well, there's actually seven subjects on the course, goys. You must have done exams at Christmas?" Oh my God, roysh, I'm storting to feel seriously dizzy. I'm like, "There's not focking seven subjects..." He's there, "There is. We're talking physiotherapy, computers, psychology..." Me and Christian are there, 'Oh my God you know what this means. If we've missed the Christmas exams, we're going to have to sit the summer repeats'. I'm like, "I am SO not cancel-ing Ocean City."

So we tell the birds, roysh, that we're going to have to postpone the flicks, because this is, like, a major emergency, and we end up hitting the sports bor, knocking back a few pints and by seven o'clock we're all totally shit-faced. We hit the M1 for a few more, then head into town to Mono. Pretty much the next thing I remember is being out on the dancefloor with the goys, giving it LOADS to Beautiful Day, roysh, and the bouncers telling us that if we can't control ourselves we're going to have to take it outside and I look around, roysh, and Fionn, who doesn't have to worry because he's doing Orts and he's focking brains to burn, he's chatting up this bird, blonde hair, big baps, a lit-tle bit like Stacey Bello, though not up close, and when I get up close she's ask-ing him where he's from and he says Killiney and she's, like, totally disgusted all of a sudden and she goes, "I am SO not getting involved in another Dorsh-line relationship" and she focks off.

And that's pretty much the last thing I can remember, except I think I ended up being with this bird Carol, who's, like, first year accountancy in Bruce, really good-looking, so like Estella Warren you'd swear it was her, but I wasn't with her for long because I could hordly stand, and I was so off-my-face I ended up giving her my number, we're talking my real number here, though that wasn't the thing I was most worried about the next morning. I don't know whether I imagined this because I was so locked and I can't get through to either of the two goys to find out whether it really happened, and anyway I think they'd already focked off at this stage, but I could have sworn, roysh, that I was walking down Grafton Street, just before I blacked out, and I bumped into Hendo, the UCD coach, who said he'd been trying to contact me all day and seeing the state of me now he's wondering why he bothered at all but I'm on the team for next week's match if I can manage to stay off the drink for that long and I'm a disgrace to the game of rugby and it's a pretty sad day for UCD that the team has to rely on the likes of me and I should get myself sobered up and get my act together and this is, like, my last big chance. And maybe it was the drink, it probably was, but I could have sworn that he said the match was against, like, Castlerock RFC. And I'm like, 'Fock'.

I text Sorcha, roysh, and it's like, "DRNK s%n? C U 2nite?" but she does-n't answer, roysh, obviously not talking to me again for who knows what rea-son.

The old man calls a meeting of KISS last week, roysh, what with all the stuff in the papers about rugby going to, like Croke Park and shit, and you SHOULD have seen our driveway. It was like focking Maxwell Motors, we're talking Beamers, Mercs, Rovers, the whole lot. The old man was, like, in his element of course, crapping on about the Berkeley Court and how the heart and soul of the game belonged to Lansdowne Road. He's there going, "I don't care whether it's Abbotstown, Croke Park or *Áras-an*-blooming-*Uachtarain*. Rugby will not be moving to the northside, certainly not as long as I have breath in my lungs and I'm chairman of Keep It South Side."

Oh my God I warned him not to make a total knob of himself again, but the old dear, roysh, she goes, "Please be on your best behaviour, Ross. Today's a big day for your father." And it must be, roysh, because the old dear's got the focking gourmet coffee out again and it's, like, I don't know, java mochacci-nos all round, and the old man's like, "It's far from Wedgwood that Bertie Ahern was reared", and everyone laughs. And the old dear, roysh, she lays the tray down on the dining-room table and goes, "For heaven's sake, the man can't even speak properly, that Bertie Ahern." And Francis, this total dick-head who's, like, president of Castlerock this year, he goes, "You're right, Fionnuala. It's all Dis, Dat, Deez and Doze with that chap." And Francis's wife is like, "C as M. The man is C as M."

The old man goes, "But we're not allowed to say that. That's why we have to think out our strategy carefully. You even mention unmarried mothers, curry chips and satellite dishes and you're immediately labeled a snob." Eduard, this complete knob the old man knows from the yacht club, he bangs his fist on the table and goes, "What are we going to do then?" And Richard, this other complete and utter dickhead who's supposed to be helping the old man get his handicap down, he goes, "That's the frustrating thing, Eduard. We know what this is about. It's about Bertie Ahern getting votes in, what is it young Tiernan calls it, Knackeragua. That's what it's about... I mean some of these young girls, they're having these babies just for the money. Are we just going to sit back and accept that that's right?"

The old man goes, "I think you've gone off on a bit of a tangent there, Richard, but your point will be noted in the minutes". I'm sitting in the next room, listening to all this bullshit. The old man goes, "But if we're to accept that we can't include anything about lycra tracksuits, sovereign rings and newsprint moustaches in our argument, then I believe there's only one way for us to fight this nonsense. And that's by using the only language that Fianna Fáil understands." Simon, who's, like, the old man's solicitor, he goes, "I can raise a few hundred thousand. Might mean going to Guernsey, but it's feasible." Eduard's like, "You'd do that?" And Simon goes, "This is an attack on our way of life, Eduard. I'd do that and a lot more besides." Richard goes, "I've known Frank Dunlop for many, many years, and something tells me that simple bribery isn't going to work this time."

Eduard, roysh, he jumps up and goes, "Well what do you suggest we do? For thirty-five years I've been going to rugby internationals. Thirty-five years. It's the Berkeley Court. It's the Dort. It's... It's.... I mean, where is Abbotstown anyway?" Simon puts his arms around him and goes, "Who knows, Eduard. Who knows..." The old man's there, "Can I just call this meeting to order for a moment and say that I think we've gone off the point slightly. This Abbot-stown business, it's still some way down the line. The real, immediate danger at the moment comes from the GAA. If they vote to open up Croke Stadium, we could be in real danger. We'll be traveling out to north Dublin for our matches quicker than you can say 'What do you mean, you don't sell Courvoisier around here?' Now I think Richard is right. Frank Dunlop has been keeping his head down lately and who can blame him?"

Eduard goes, "Kerrigan. He hates anyone with money…" The old man's like, "Let me finish, Eduard. What I'm saying is let's deal with the GAA first. If we need to bribe anyone, we've got to get a few of these Gaelic Association of… What does it stand for? Gaelic… I don't know, these GAA chaps. What I'm saying is let's put together, say, £50,000 each and try to bribe a few of them. Get them to vote against it." Simon goes, "Just think of all the bacon and cabbage and, I don't know, sports coats they could buy for that kind of money." And Richard's like, "We can offer it to them, but they'd never go for it, would they?"

JP, roysh, he persuades Oisínn to borrow his old man's car, we're talking a big fock-off Beamer here, and they head out to Tallaghtfornia, and they drive around some real skanger estate, with JP sticking his head out through the sunroof, just shouting, "AFFLUENCE. AFFLUENCE."

Amanda, roysh, this bird who I have to say has the total hots for me, a friend of Eanna's sister, I saw this morning at the bus stop in, like, Stillorgan, waiting for the 46a, so, like, I pulled over, roysh, asked her does she want a lift into college and she's like, "Oh my God, you are SUCH a life-saver" and I'm there, "Hey, it's a pleasure to have such a beautiful woman in my car," playing it totally Kool and the Gang. We're getting on really well, roysh. She tells me all about this huge row she's just had with her parents because her old man – a complete dickhead apparently – is refusing to pay her car insurance and then about some friend of hers who's on the permanent guest list in Reynards. So anyway, to cut a long story short, roysh, we get to UCD and she says she so has to, like, buy me lunch to say thank you, giving it loads, TOTALLY gagging for me. So I arrange to meet her in the Orts block, roysh. She's in, like, first year, we're talking Philosophy and, like, Linguistics, which is what she had that morning. I know because I basically just hung around waiting for her, roysh, but then I got bored so I ended up, like, going into her lecture. She's sitting in the back row, roysh, with a couple of her mates, one of them I recognise from Club Shoot-Your-Goo, and she sort of, like, mouths the word Hi! to me and I scooch up beside her. The lecturer, roysh, he is SO boring bastard it's unbelievable. He's like, "In English, a double negative is a positive. In some languages, including Russian, the inverse is also the case, but there is no incidence in the English language where a double positive forms a negative." I'm like, "Yeah, roysh!" And everyone breaks their shites laughing, roysh, and I didn't even realise I'd, like, said it so loud, and I look at Amanda and her head is turned the other way and I can hear her going, "Oh my God I'm so embarrassed."

Valentine's Day was the usual crack, got four cords: two from, like, secret admirers, roysh, one from Jessica Heaney who's, like, second year Actuarial and Financial Studies in UCD, a big-time flirt, so like Natasha Henstridge you'd swear they were twins, and one other which was addressed to "the goy with the smallest penis in UCD", which is obviously from Keeva or Amy or some other bird I've given the flick to and is having a problem getting over it, maybe Emma or Sinéad. Or Cara or Jill. One of those orseholes.

Anyway, roysh, Oisínn got his hands on tickets for the Valentine's Ball, so there I am in my gaff getting ready, roysh, looking pretty well I have to say in my new beige chinos, light blue Ralph and docksiders, when all of a sudden there's this, like, ring at the door. I open it, roysh, and surprise su-focking-prise, who is it only Sorcha, who hands me this cord, roysh, and this present and goes, "Friends?", and I just, like, shrug my shoulders and go, "Whatever." Then she gives me this, like, hug and goes, "You smell SO nice. What are you wearing?" Everything with this girl comes with a focking hug. I'm like, "Emporio He" and she goes, "Giorgio Armani?" and I just, like, nod at her.

She's, like, totally dressed to kill, roysh, and we're talking totally here, and she's there going, "Are you going out tonight?" and I'm there, "I'm going to the Valentine's Ball" and she goes, "Oh my God where is it on this year?" and I just go, "Town." She is SO trying to get in with me it's not funny, roysh. She's like, "Are you not going to open your present?" so I tear open the wrapping and it's, like, the new U2 album, which I've basically wanted for ages and she goes, "I hope you haven't already got it", and I'm like, "Yeah, I have actually", and she says oh my God she'll change it but I tell her not to bother, that I'll give it to Megan and she's like, "Who's Megan?" and I'm like, "This girl I've been seeing.

She's, like, first year B and L. You wouldn't know her, she looks like Holly Valance", completely making it up and the sad bitch nearly bursts into tears.

The next thing, roysh, the old dear decides to stick her focking oar in, she comes out to the hall and goes, "Sorcha, come in, come in", and the two of them disappear off into the kitchen, roysh, talking about the sale in focking Pamela Scott and whether or not Ikea will ever open up a branch in Dublin. I just, like, grab the cor keys. The old dear tells me to drive carefully and I tell her to focking cop herself on and as I'm leaving I notice that Sorcha has actually got, like, tears in her eyes and she's hordly even touched the cappuccino the old dear's made for her and I'm like, What a total spa.

The Coyote Lounge is totally jammers, roysh. There's, like, a queue halfway up focking D'Olier Street when we arrive and everyone's there going, "WE HATE C&E. WE HATE C&E", and the commerce and economics society goys are, like, totally bulling. After about an hour, roysh, we finally manage to get inside, but I end up having a pretty shit night, probably because I'm only drinking Diet Coke. The only bit of crack I actually have, roysh, is watching Oisínn totally crash and burn when he chances his orm with Phenola, this complete fruitcake who's, like, second year B&L. He's chatting away to her, roysh, giving it loads, and that Destiny's Child song comes on, roysh, *Independent Woman*, music for cutting men's mickeys off to, and all of a sudden he makes a lunge for her, but she, like, slaps him across the face and tells him that trying to be with a girl while that song is playing is SUCH a no-no. It's, like, SO funny seeing this big six-foot-five, seventeen-stone prop forward getting slapped across the face by this little, like, squirt of a girl.

But then I end up getting cornered by Katie, roysh, this total knob who's, like, first year Orts, and we end up having one of those pain-in-the-orse conversations which storts off with her asking me who I know in Orts and I go, "Lisa Andrews", and she goes, "Oh my God I can't BELIEVE you know Lisa Andrews. She's one of my best friends. Who else?" And I go, "James O'Hagan", and she goes, "Oh my God I can't BELIEVE you know James O'Hagan. I was with him at the Freshers Frolic." I'm storting to lose the focking will to live when Fionn comes over and rescues me, roysh, and he points over to this bird, I think it's Blathnaid, who's, like, repeating first year Counselling and Psychotherapy in LSB, and she's wearing half-nothing, and Fionn turns around to me and goes, "Gardaí at Harcourt Terrace are seeking the public's help in tracing the whereabouts of Bláthnaid Brady's clothes." I laugh, roysh, but I tell him then that I'm going to fock off home, what with me having to be up early the next morning.

The next day was a pretty big one for me. Castlerock were playing their first match in the Senior Cup against, like, Templeogue – they totally kicked orse – and Feely asked me to go back and give the goys on the S, like, pep-talk and shit. I have to say I was pretty nervous going back, roysh, especially with all the shit that's going on over next week's match. Pretty much everyone will have heard that I'm playing for College, roysh, and our game next week is against I think I mentioned Castlerock RFC, with mid-table mediocrity in Division Two of the AIL at stake. It's a mare. A total one.

The club actually made me a pretty decent offer when I finished school, roysh, and of course I went down, checked out the facilities and shit, but then I got offered the sports scholarship and basically decided to take it. Anyway, as it turns out, roysh, I'd nothing to worry about, because I got an amazing reception at the school. I'm there giving the goys on the S my speech, roysh, all that, "THIS IS THE GAME OF YOUR LIVES" and "KICK ORSE, ROCK", roysh, and as I'm leaving the stage, the whole assembly is there singing, "Castlerock Über Alles" and it's really emotional, but then Magahy, one of the geography teachers, he comes up to me, roysh, and asks whether it's true that I'm going to be playing against Castlerock in the AIL next week.

Now this goy, roysh, is a total dickhead, coached the junior cup team when I was in first year, and is a total club man, going to all the matches, sitting up at the bor, thinking he knows everything about rugby when in fact he knows fock-all. I totally hate this goy. When I was in, like, second year, roysh, I missed a pretty simple penalty and we ended up getting knocked out of the junior cup by focking Pres Bray, of all schools, and Magahy goes to me, as I'm leaving the pitch, "You're going to be huge, Ross... Especially if you keep eating the way you do." I so haven't forgotten that. Anyway, roysh, he turns to me this day and he goes, "So you're going to be a turncoat then?" and I just, like, straighten my baseball cap, roysh, and go, "No, Magahy, you dickhead. I'm going to be focking sensational."

If only I could get Erika into my cor or anywhere I could put on the *Pretty Woman* tape.

Simon is the first one over. He comes up to me, roysh, and he goes, "So it's true then?" I'm like, "What's true?" and he goes, "You ARE a focking turncoat." I'm there, "You are SUCH a sad bastard." He goes, "I seriously didn't think you'd play" and he, like, pushes me in the chest, roysh, and calls me a turncoat again and I, like, switch my gearbag to my other shoulder, basically getting ready to deck the focker if he touches me again, but then he storts going, like, totally ballistic and I mean totally. He's there, "Whatever happened to Castlerock above all others? We'll shy from battle never? Ein volk, ein Reich, ein Rock?"

I'm just there, "We're not at school anymore, Simon. I'm playing for UCD now." He storts, like, shaking his head, roysh, going, "No, no, no", we're talking tears in his eyes, the whole lot, and he's there, "You NEVER leave Castlerock, Ross. And IT never leaves you." I'm trying to reason with the goy, roysh, telling him that playing for UCD is, like, one of the conditions of my scholarship and shit. But he keeps bullshitting on about how pretty much all of the goys off the S went on to sign for Castlerock and now, just when they're looking like pulling themselves out of the bottom four of the second division of the AIL, along comes one of their own to stab them in the back. He goes, "You haven't played rugby all season, Ross." I'm there, "Yeah, that's why I've got a point to prove. Show them that the old magic is still there." He goes, "But why now? Why this game?" I go, "I've grown up, Simon. I think it's about time you did too," and I stort, like, heading towards the dressing-rooms and he shouts after me that I'm totalled, totally focking totalled and he's talking totally.

I get into the dressing-room and all the other goys are already there and Hendo, our coach, is giving this, like, major peptalk about how we've, like, striven all season to finish mid-table and we can't let it slip through our fingers now. He tells us all, roysh, to think about the sacrifices we've made for this game and I stort thinking about Wednesday night, roysh, and the C&E Mystery Tour and how I ended up staying sober for the entire evening in some boozer in focking Athboy and, even though Julianne, this total knob who's, like, second year commerce, borfed her ring up all over my jacket on the bus on the way there, I still didn't drink, that's how up for this game I am. I'm getting changed into my gear, roysh, when Hendo storts, like, looking at me, roysh, and he goes, "Any divided loyalties here today?" and I'm there, "Are you talking to me?" And he goes, "I saw you talking to Simon. I just want to know whether you're with us or against us today?" I'm just there, "I'm kicking focking orse today," and the whole dressing-room goes ballistic, roysh, everyone banging the lockers, kicking the walls and going, "YOU THE MAN, ROSS. YOU THE MAN".

It's just like the old days, roysh, except that outside the door there's a couple of hundred Castlerock fans giving me total filthies when we go out instead of, like, cheering me on, but I do see one friendly face in the crowd and it's, like, Christian, roysh, and I walk up to him and go, "Hey, Christian. Looks like I'm public enemy number one around here." He goes, "Anyone hurts you out there today, man, and I'll focking kill them." I'm there, "I knew you'd understand. Us College heads have to stick together, eh?" He goes, "No. That doesn't mean I'm on your side, Ross. I won't stand by and watch you get hurt, but that doesn't mean I agree with what you've done." I'm like, "What have I done, Christian?" He goes, "You've turned to the dark side." Then he unzips his jacket, roysh, we're talking his red and blue Armani sailing jacket here, and underneath it he's got his old Castlerock jersey and he just looks me up and down and goes, "The Emperor has won", and he walks off. I can see, like, Fionn and JP and Oisínn, all those, over the other side of the pitch and they're, like, giving me filthies and we're talking total filthies.

Out on the pitch, roysh, all the old goys are there, we're talking Eunan, Jonathon, Brad, Evan, Newer, Gicker, and I try to shut it out of my mind as the game storts, roysh, and I do pretty well, getting seven out of my eight kicks and putting in what I have to say is an amazing tackle on Simon when he's, like, clean through for a certain try. At half-time we're, like, 21-13 up, but the Castlerock goys stort to tackle me really hord in the second half, there's total focking hatred there, and I sort of, like, go off my game a bit, miss a couple of, like, pretty easy kicks and suddenly Castlerock stort to get on top of us. Simon's having a focking stormer.

Two minutes to go and it's, like, 33-27 for them, roysh, and we pretty much need a seven-pointer to win it. We're pressing, pressing, pressing, in the last few minutes, roysh, and suddenly the ball breaks to me and I get over for a try right under the post and there's all this, like, booing right the way around the ground. All the goys on our team are coming up to me congratulating me, roysh, but also reminding me how important the kick is, as if I need reminding. As I'm walking back to take it, roysh, Christian runs onto the pitch, comes right up to me and goes, "I know there's good in you. I've felt it", and eventually a couple of stewards come on and drag him away.

The kick is a piece of piss. I blow hord, take three steps backwards and three to the left, run my hand through my hair, blow hord again. I look over at

Simon and Eunan, who have their hands on the crests of their jersey, we're talking tears in their focking eyes here. I look at Christian, roysh, who's got his eyes closed, like he's praying or some shit. I look at Jim Foy, the Castlerock chairman who got me a summer job in the bank last year and told me if I ever needed work to, like, give him a shout. I run my hand through my hair and, like, blow hord again. And then I send the kick high and wide and in the direction of the corner flag.

Sophie says she's been asked to go back to her old school, roysh, we're talking Loreto Foxrock here, to play the piano for Goys and Dolls, which they're doing with, like, Blackrock College, and it's because Rebecca Ryan has, like, glandular fever, roysh, but OH MY GOD, she goes, we will NEVER guess who's pissed off about that, Sara Cavanagh, Sara with no H Cavanagh, we're talking Melissa Cavanagh's little sister? She SO wanted to do it but basically she's not good enough, she goes, and Miss Hempenstall SO knows that.

Aoife says she's thinking of getting chocolate ice cream and she asks is anyone else having dessert. No one answers. Oisínn is texting JP to tell him he scored Gemma Halvey in Peg's last night, Gemma Halvey or Elizabeth Arden Fifth Avenue as he calls her. Chloë asks Sophie whether she's been talking to Erika and Sophie says not since last Saturday when she met her in town and OH my God you SHOULD have seen the chainmail neckpiece she got in Morgan, it was SO gorgeous. Chloë says she heard that Erika's not actually going away for the summer and she's, like, so lucky, because it means she'll be here for the Horse Show, although Chloë says that for her 19th she's going to ask her dad for the fare to basically fly back from Montauk for it and Sophie says that is SUCH a good idea. Aoife goes, "I'm definitely getting ice cream. Sophie, you'll get ice cream as well won't you?"

Oisínn finishes texting JP and asks the girls whether they're interested in going away for Easter, maybe renting a gaff in, like, Galway or something and Chloë says no way, especially after that whole New Year in Inishbofin, oh MY God what a total disaster she goes, and Oisínn asks her what happened, roysh, and she says the woman who ran the B&B didn't take Visa, oh my God, she says, can you ACTUALLY believe that, she didn't take any credit cord and there wasn't, like, an ATM on the island or anything.

Aoife goes, "Come on, I don't want to be the only one getting dessert." Sophie asks Chloë how Julian is, roysh, and Chloë says he's still upset about the break-up and she's told him it's going to, like, take time to get over it and Oisínn asks her whether Julian is a faggot and Chloë gives him this filthy and I, like, suddenly stort showing an interest in my mobile phone. Chloë goes, "Why did you ask that?" and Oisínn's like, "Because everyone knows that if you call your kid Julian or Quentin or one of those names, there's a fairly high chance that he's going to, like, turn out gay." Chloë goes, "Have you got something against people who are gay?" and Oisínn's like, "No", and Chloë, roysh, she's just there, "You better not have. I've got LOADS of friends who are gay."

Oisínn mutters under his breath, he's there, "Yep, he's bent alright." Aoife goes, "Chloë, if I get ice cream, will you share it with me?"

This bitch in front of me, roysh, is SO trying to fock me over it's unbelievable. We're coming up to the lights in Donnybrook, roysh, and I'm right up her orse I have to admit, but there's this, like, yellow box on the ground and she goes through it and then, like, stops just on the other side of it, which basically means that I have to stop INSIDE the box and now all of a sudden the lights are red for us and there's, like, traffic coming the other way but they can't, like, get past because I'm in the focking box and they're all, like, beeping me, but I can't move. All because of this bitch. And the next thing, roysh, my mobile rings and I answer it and it's, like, Amy, this bird who's in philosophy with Aoife who has the big-time hots for me, and even though I say I can't talk right now she totally ignores me and tells me she was in Lillies last night and OH MY GOD I will not believe who was, we're talking Phil Babb and the two Carter Twins as well. I listen to her shit for, like, ten seconds and then I hang up and some dickhead in front of me in a blue Alfa Romeo obviously doesn't know that this road is two lanes, he's driving up the middle, roysh, and I just keep flashing him and he eventually pulls over into, of all places, the focking fast lane, even though he's only doing, like, thirty miles an hour or something and then he pulls level with this goy in the inside lane, some knob in a red Renault Mégane, and he storts driving at exactly the same speed as him, so I can't overtake him. I'm just there, like, giving him the finger. And Karen Shue, roysh, she says the lights are ait of action at the junction of Stephen's Green and Leeson Streesh and there's bad delays around Thomas Streesh and James's Streesh and an accident to watch ait for on the Old Court Raid and the lights are out at Amiens Streesh, Store Streesh and Botanic Avenue and on the Carysfort Raid at the Rock Raid junction. And I still can't get anything decent on the radio and it's all m-commerce whatever the fock that is, and past performance is no guarantee of future returns and now you can talk on the phone while surfing the net and The Corrs and Emma focking Bunton and the market is apparently eroding the value of technology stocks and Gateway is the latest company to issue a profit warning...

I'm on the 46a, roysh, TRYING to have a conversation with Fionn when all of a sudden we're going through Stillorgan, roysh, all these knobs from Coláiste Iosagáin get on and stort, like, talking in Irish, or that's what JP said it was anyway, but oh my God they are SO wrecking my head it's unbelievable. I'm there, "What the fock are they trying to say?" And JP, who actually did grinds, he goes, "I can't be sure, it's a dialect I don't quite understand, but they seem to be talking about the teachers' strike." I couldn't understand why they were looking so focking miserable then. They actually seemed to be disappointed that they might not get to do the Leaving and I'm there wishing there was a focking lecturers strike. Four weeks until the exams and I still haven't done a tap. I am SO going to have to repeat at this stage it's not funny, which is why I'm going out on the lash tonight, to try to forget about it. Of course, it's alright for JP, he's working for his old man, who's, like, an estate agent. He turns around to me, roysh, and goes, "Will your old pair flip when they find out you're going to fail?" and I'm just like, "Totally."

I'm supposed to be going to Ocean City for the summer, roysh, and I'll be SO pissed off if I have to come back to sit the repeats, so I tell JP that I'm thinking of just repeating the whole year, maybe actually going to a few lectures next year and I'm trying to get my head around all of this, roysh, but all around me it's all, "Tá me, tá me, conas atá tú, blah blah blah" and I turn around to these two knobs behind me and I go, "There's no focking Leaving Cert this year. Get over it" and one of them, roysh, she turns back to me and she goes, "Sorry, would you mind your own business please?" And quick as a flash, roysh, I turn around and go, "Only if you get a focking life." Then I'm like, "Talking in that stupid focking language on the bus. School's over. HELLO?"

I turn around, roysh, expecting JP to, like, back me up, but instead he's chatting away to these other two girls in front of us, telling them that it's the students he feels sorry for and that he's thinking of applying to become an exam supervisor. The girls think this is "SO cool", the smooth bastard. I don't know which of the two he's trying to be with, roysh, but I can't watch and I decide to get off in, like, Donnybrook and see are any of the goys in Kiely's. As I'm heading down the stairs, roysh, I can hear him arranging to meet the girls in some pub in town after the Institute. The focker hasn't even noticed I've gone.

We're in town, roysh, standing in some focking nightclub queue, so off my face I don't even know the name of it, the girls giving out yords to me and Christian telling us to sober up big-time or we're so not going to get in. Emer says that if we don't all get in here we should head to Lillies and Sophie says she was there last night and oh my God Jason Sherlock was in there and so was Liz What's-her-name from *Off The Rails*. Emer asks her who she went with and Sophie says Alyson with a y and Emer asks if it's true that Alyson with a y is going to Australia for the year and Sophie goes, "When she finishes in Mountjoy Square, yeah." Erika shoots Emer a filthy, roysh, why I don't know, but then again Erika never needs, like, a reason.

We get up to the door and there's no way the bouncers are going to let us in, me and Christian are SO struggling to hold it together, we're totally hanging, especially Christian who was really hitting the sauce tonight, but Sophie, roysh, she goes, "Oh my God, I think I know one of the goys on the door", and when we get up to the front of the queue she, like, flashes a smile at this big focking gorilla, goes, "Hi-how-or-ya?" and then gives him a peck on the cheek and a hug. The goy hasn't a clue who she is but he goes along with it, roysh, he's getting his thrills, the old sly-hand-on-the-orse routine. He goes, "You smell lovely tonight, girls". He's a total focking howiya.

Sophie goes, "Oh my God I've put make-up on your shirt," and she storts, like, rubbing his collar, roysh, but the goy goes, "Don't worry about it. You can put make-up on me any time you like, love", and all the girls laugh, roysh, all except Erika, who is so not impressed, and she's got, like, her arms folded, really pissed off at being kept waiting. Of course the bouncer, roysh, he pushes it too far. He goes to hug her next, and I so want to deck the focker at this stage, but she doesn't respond, roysh, and it's like he's hugging an ironing board or something, and when he pulls away, roysh, she asks him what the fock he thinks he's doing and he says he's just being friendly, and Erika goes, "You are SO sexually frustrated. Why don't you just get a dirty magazine, go to the little boys' room and stop making a nuisance of yourself out here."

I would SO love to know what Sorcha's game is. She hasn't spoken to me for, like, a whole week, but she texts me today and it's like, "DRINK 2NITE?" She is SO focking with my head at the moment. I text her back and I'm like, "C U QUEENS @ 8."

Sophie phones me up, bawling her eyes out, roysh, telling me she failed philosophy and her parents are going to go ballistic and OH MY GOD her old man is so NOT going to give her the money to go skiing now, and it's all because of that complete dickhead of a lecturer who set SUCH a hard paper, everyone said so, even Wendy, and he was SUCH an asshole to her when she went to him to try to get her grade changed, roysh, and I can just picture her going in to see him in her little titty-top trying to sweet-talk the goy. She tells me she SO needs someone to talk to and can I come over, roysh, and I'm pretty much certain of getting my bit, so I'm there, 'Is the bear a Catholic?' I'm actually on the way back from Christian's gaff, roysh, and I'm pretty much home, but I turn the car around and head for Glenageary. Oh MY God, she goes, it wasn't like she was looking for a 2.1 or even a 2.2, all she wanted was a scabby pass and he was too much of a focking asshole to give her that and oh my God her points have, like, totally gone out the window, because she's eaten, like, three bars of Dairy Millk, which is 18 points in itself and that's all she's supposed to have in an entire day and that's not even counting the Weight Watchers lasagne, we're talking the beef one, not the vegetarian, which is, like, five-and-a-half, the four pieces of Ryvita which is, like, two, and the bowl of Fruit and Fibre which is, like, one-and-a-half or five-and-a-half if you have it with full milk, which she did. She goes oh my God it was bad enough failing without going into that DICKHEAD and making a complete spa of herself and she tells me she asked the goy what he would suggest she do, roysh, and he told her to, like, set her sights lower, maybe get a job with FM104 or one of the other radio stations driving one of those big four-wheel drives around town. He said he was sure that a girl with her talent would be snapped up quickly.

# Chapter Four

*The one where Ross wears a polo-neck*

HAZEL is this bird I met in the M1, roysh, a Montessori teacher and a total lasher, we're talking SO like Rachael Leigh Cook it's not funny. I was, like, sitting up at the bor with Christian and Fionn, roysh, just talking about rugby and shit when her and a couple of her friends – recognized one of them from The Palace, Orna is her name, second year law in Portobello – they came up and they were ordering drinks, roysh, and Orna picks up Fionn's mobile phone and storts, like, scrolling down through all the names in his directory, going, "Keavo? Oh my God is that Alan Keaveney?" I turned around to Hazel, who was paying for, like, two vodka and Red Bulls and a Smirnoff Ice, roysh, and storted chatting away to her, working the old charm on her.

I asked her what Montessori school actually was, roysh, but of course I was too busy thinking of my next line to listen properly to what she was saying, though from what I could make out it's pretty much the same as, like, a normal nursery school, except that instead of giving the kids, like, paint and jigsaws and shit, they teach them focking Japanese and how to play, like, the violin. Of course, I'm there pretending to be really interested. End of the night, roysh, Christian's focked off home, because his old man moved out of the house today and he wants to make sure his old dear is alright, I mean I tried to go with him but he said he wanted to be on his own, so it's, like, just me, Fionn, Orna and Hazel left. Orna is completely off her tits, roysh, and she keeps telling us she has to have an essay in for Tort tomorrow and she hasn't done a tap on it and she is SO dead it's unbelievable. Eventually, roysh, Fionn leans over to me and goes, "I'm going to drop the Chief Justice here home" and I high-five him and he helps her off the stool and out the door and Hazel, roysh, she shows no sign of going home with her friend, so obviously I'm

there going, "I am SO in here." I'm there, "So, where are you living?" still playing it Kool and the Gang. She goes, "Sandycove." I'm like, "I've been known to
find myself in that particular vicinity. Can I drive you home. We're talking
Golf GTI. Black. With alloys", and she goes, "Cool."

We're heading out towards her gaff, roysh, and I decide it's time to put on
the old *Pretty Woman* tape, but I can't remember whether I've, like, rewound
the tape to the stort of 'Fallen'. If I haven't, roysh, she's going to hear Roy Orbison singing the focking title track, which is actually a pretty good song but a
total passion killer, so I'm, like, taking a bit of a chance pressing the play button, but it's cool because the next thing I hear is Lauren Wood and Hazel goes,
"Oh my God I don't believe it." I'm like, "What?" and she goes, "Oh my God
this HAS to be fate. This is, like, my favourite song of all time." I'm like, "Really? Who is it, Samantha Mumba?" cracking on I don't know. She goes, "It's
from *Pretty Woman*. Is this a tape?" I'm like, "No, it's just the radio" and she
goes, "Oh my God then it is fate. Every time I hear this song I'm going to think
of you now." If only she knew how many locks I've picked with this tape.

So we pull up outside her gaff, roysh, massive pad, and she goes, "Oh my
God I said I wouldn't let this happen?" I'm like, "Let what happen?" She goes,
"I promised myself that I wouldn't fall so easily again. Especially after Cian."
I'm like, "Who's Cian," as if I give a shit. She goes, "You don't want to know."
She's right there, but then she's like, "I got really hurt. I don't know what to
do." I'm like, "Just go with the flow," and I move in for the kill, roysh, but as I
go to kiss her she goes, "What are you doing?" I'm like, "Hey, a little bit of
what you fancy is good for you." I hate myself for using Oisínn's chat-up lines,
but it doesn't work anyway and she pushes me away, just as Roy Orbison
comes on as it happens, and I'm thinking that she maybe has, like, a starring
role in a period costume drama, but she says it's just that she wants to, like,
take things a bit more slowly? So it looks as though this could be a two-day
job, which under normal circumstances, roysh, would be enough to put me
off completely, but she asks me what I'm doing tomorrow night and of course
I've now got to face that, like, dilemma – do I cut my losses now and just tell
her I'm busy or do I agree to have a second crack at it, which I never really do
with girls. One thing is certain, roysh, this whole taking-things-a-bit-more-
slowly shit sounds like she has a potential relationship on her mind and even
though I know it's a mistake I end up giving her my number, my actual real
number, and she says she'll, like, give me a call the next day.

Which she does, the sap. She rings me at, like, eleven the next morning, roysh, a bit too John B as Fionn would say, and asks me whether I fancy going, like, bowling? I'm like, bowling? HELLO? I must have been pretty sloshed the night before not to notice what a total knob this girl is, but she caught me unawares. I was still in the focking scratcher when she rang, so I ended up agreeing to meet her in Stillorgan, roysh, and that afternoon I'm pulling into the cor pork, roysh, thinking, 'If any of the goys find out I'm bowling with a bird, I'm history.' Unbeknownst to me, of course, she's bringing her whole focking class with her, we're talking a school trip here, with me roped in as a focking child minder for the day. We are talking total mortification.

I'm in such a fouler I end up having a row with the bird who, like, gives out those crappy shoes. First of all, roysh, she said I couldn't wear my dock-siders, even though they've got, like, white soles. She goes, "You have to use the house shoes," these half-red, half-blue things that make you look like a complete knob. And then, roysh, she tells me she needs a deposit of, like, five notes? I'm like, "HELLO? I've just handed you a pair of shoes that cost eighty bills. They're focking Dubarry. Do you honestly think I'm going to run off with these focking things?" and I point down to my feet, roysh, but she just goes, "That will be five pound, sir", like she's a focking robot or something.

And the kids, roysh, they were all little shits, brilliant at bowling of course, every focking one of them. And Hazel keeps coming up to me going, "Oh my God you are SO good with kids", obviously marking me down as marriage material – I'm there going, 'Do not even GO there, girl' – and she mustn't have seen me whacking one of the little spoilt shits around the ear. The little focker kicked me, roysh, and told me I was rubbish at bowling, so I hit him a sly little slap around the head, the kind the referee never sees, then bent one of his fingers back and told him he was a spoiled little brat, and of course he goes bawling his eyes out to Hazel, who is such a sad bitch she actually believes me when I tell her he caught his fingers in the bowling ball, and the kid stays out of my way for the rest of the day, the clever boy.

Then, roysh, it's all across the road to McDonalds, me trying to talk to Hazel to find out if I've any focking chance of scoring at the end of all this, and her reminding me to keep my eyes on the ten or eleven little shits who are walking behind us. I feel like the old woman who lived in the focking shoe, sitting there in the restaurant with all these little fockers running around me. And they're all going, "Are you Hazel's boyfriend?" And this one kid, roysh, he sucks a load of Coke up into his straw, roysh, and I swear to God the little shit's about to, like, spit it at me and I'm like, "DON'T YOU..." And Hazel all of a sudden jumps up and goes, "NO ROSS!" I'm like, "What?" She goes, "You're not allowed to use the D word to the young people." I'm like, "What D word?" She goes, "The D-O-N-Apostrophe-T word. It's a Montessori thing, Ross. You're not allowed to say don't or can't to the young people. They're negatives, you see." I'm like, "So what do you do then, just slap them?" She looks at me totally horrified, like I've got, like, ten heads or something. She goes, "You shouldn't hit young people, Ross. Nobody should live in fear of violence. When you're trying to stop a young person from acting in an anti-social way, you have to acknowledge that emotions are involved. So to stop Lorcan from spitting his drink at you, what you should say is, 'I understand why you want to do that and I understand that you are upset that I'm asking you not to do it, but I really feel that...'" As she's saying this, roysh, the little focker sitting next to Lorcan is squashing gherkin into the table. I just get up to go, roysh, wave at Hazel and go, "*Arrivederci*," which, I remember on the way home, isn't actually Japanese, but I'm sure she got the message anyway.

I get a call from this bird in RTE, roysh, and she tells me that she got my name off a friend of mine who said I was, like, amazing at rugby, and she asked whether I'd be interested in working on *Rapid* as, like, a guest presenter for a couple of weeks because, like, Jason Sherlock's sick. I'm like, "Cool". She asks me, roysh, whether I've done any television work before and I tell her no, except a couple of interviews with Ryle Nugent and it turns out, roysh, that it was he who recommended me. He went to Blackrock and he's friends with Al, Fionn's cousin.

So I goes out to Donnybrook a few days later, roysh, and this bird tells me that we're going to be filming a skills feature with, like, Brian O'Driscoll, and of course I'm there going, "Cool", because I have to say, roysh, he's actually a bit of a hero of mine, a very good rugby player and totally sound as well. It's pretty embarrassing, roysh, because we turn up on the day we're supposed to do the filming in exactly the same clothes, except that his chinos were, like, Ralph Lauren and mine were, like, Dockers. Anyway, roysh, it sort of helps to break the ice, because I could tell he was, like, pretty nervous meeting me.

So we head out to the back pitch at Lansdowne Road to do the filming and you should have seen the filthies the camera crew gave me when I turned around to Brian and went, "Okay, what skills do you want me to teach you?"

Turns out, roysh, it was supposed to be the other way around? He was supposed to be teaching me? I'm not being big-headed or anything, but I'm like, HELLO? Although I have to say, roysh, I ended up just playing along with it, I mean I so didn't want to embarrass the goy.

Fionn rings, roysh, and he storts blabbing on about some bird from, like, third year Commerce with French, who he ended up being with at the B&L ball the other night and I'm just there, "Whatever", and he asks me whether I got his text message and I tell him I'll have to ring him back later because some BITCH in a green Seat Ibiza is SO trying to fock me over. She's, like, turning left into the garage on Booterstown Avenue, roysh, and she's going SO slow that I have to drop down to third gear and I'm like, "Oh my God, you are SO lucky I'm in a hurry". And the traffic is, like, WHAT THE FOCK is the point of having a cor that can go this fast if you can only get to, like, fifty and suddenly you're driving up someone's orse...

Sorcha gives me this look, roysh, we're talking total daggers here, and she goes, "Ross, spare me the character dissection". I'm like, "I only asked what you thought of my baseball cap" and she goes, "Can we please change the subject?" I nod at the borman, roysh, and he takes this as a signal that we want the same again and the lounge girl brings over a pint of Heino and, like, a Diet Coke. I'm there, "Thanks for meeting me" and she goes, "We're friends. When Dawson and Joey broke up, that didn't stop them having their movie nights, did it?" I'm like, "No", even though I haven't a focking clue what she's talking about. She tells me she's, like, so chilled out these days and it's SO because of the music she's been listening to. She tells me she had Tchaikovsky's *Scene from Swan Lake* on in the car on the way in and Bizet's *Au Fond Du Temple Saint*, and even though the third CD takes a lot of getting used to she's really started getting into Strauss, Holst, Prokofiev and Copland. I tell her I've been mostly listening to Eminen, the new U2 album, a bit of Oasis, and she tells me my taste is SO up my orse it's unbelievable and she offers to lend me her *Saving Private Ryan* soundtrack, which she says is SO easy to listen to and SUCH a good way to get into classical music, especially

*Hymn To The Fallen, Wade's Death* and *Omaha Beach,* and I'm like, "Cool."

She stubs out a Marlboro Light, lights another and goes, "You heard about Sophie's exams then?" and I'm like, "Yeah she was a bit freaked about them." She goes, "She said you called over to her that night. She said you were very nice to her." I'm like, "Eh, yeah." She's there, "How nice?" And I'm there, "What do you care?" and she starts breaking her shite laughing and goes, "I'm only teasing you, silly." I'm like, "You're jealous, aren't you?" and she goes, "Don't flatter yourself, Ross. Do NOT flatter yourself."

I start slagging her then, roysh, for being late and she goes, "HELLO? I texted you", but I must have accidentally, like, switched my phone off because when I turn it on there's a message from her and it's like, "IL B l8. 20 MINS. C U l8r". And she looks so, like, smug as she takes off her scrunchy, slips it onto her wrist, shakes her hair free and then smoothes it back into a low ponytail again, puts it back in the scrunchy and then pulls five or six, like, strands of hair loose again. She goes, "I think you owe me an apology, Ross", and then she smiles as though she knows she's not going to, like, get one.

She tells me that her and Aoife are thinking of going to Australia for the year, then she asks me if I heard about Sadbh and Macker and I tell her no and she says they broke up, which is SUCH a pity because they looked SO cute together even though they were so not suited, and I agree, even though I don't know who she's talking about because I can never really work out whether she's talking about real life or, like, some American programme she watches, but I agree with her because when we're getting on like this Sorcha is so easy to talk to.

I ask her whether she wants a drink and she says it's her round, roysh, and when she comes back from the bor she asks me how Christian is. I tell her his old man's moved out and she goes, "Mum said he's living in Dalkey, in the apartment they own". I'm like, "Christian won't go and see him." She goes, "He's taking it really bad, isn't he?" I can't really answer that. I find it, like, hord to talk to goys about shit like that when I'm sober, roysh, and whenever I'm locked, Christian is always twice as bad and pretty much impossible to talk to. I've thought about sending him maybe, like, a text message. Sort of like, "R U OK?" but it just doesn't, like, seem enough? I'm there, "The States will take his mind off it, I think." She tells me he's SO lucky to have a friend like me and even though she means it she's wrong. I tell her she's looking well and she tells me that's the third time I've said that tonight.

"Ross, I cannot believe you're wearing a polo-neck in this weather. And a black polo-neck at that." The old dear says this to me at the dinner table, roysh, and I'm just there, you know, yeah whatever, but she just will not let it go, roysh, and it's like she knows the focking reason I'm wearing it and she's trying to, like, embarrass the shit out of me? "The hottest day of the year and you decide to wear something like that," she goes. "Charles, say something to Ross, will you?" The old man is just, like, staring at the back page of the *Sunday Independent*, going, "Kerrigan... What's he AFTER". The old dear's like, "Put away the paper, darling. Come on, it's salmon-*en-croute*", and then she turns to me, roysh, and goes, "and Ross, why don't you go upstairs and change into a T-shirt. I've ironed your Ralph what-do-you-call-it. Much more appropriate for a day like today. Get some colour into you." I'm just there, "Will you just shut up going on about it. You are SUCH a knob, do you know that? And I get up from the table and, like, storm out of the house and I get into the cor, roysh, Golf GTI with alloys, total babe magnet, and I check out my neck in the rear-view. Only two types of people wear polo-necks, knobs mostly and then those of us unlucky enough to have gotten a dirty big Denis on our necks in Peg's on Monday night.

I should have seen it coming, but I was completely off my face, bank holiday weekend, why not, roysh, originally went out for a few scoops, ended up, like, knocking back beers until whatever, maybe two in the morning, and what with one thing and another I ended up being with Auveen, this total babe who's, like, second year Orts, roysh, and a little bit like Piper Perabo, except with, like, braces on her teeth. Anyway, roysh, the goys, well Fionn mostly, he calls her The Hound of the Baskervilles because when she's, like, shit-faced, roysh, she starts, like, sucking the neck off you. Of course, Monday night, I was too off my face to fight her off.

So I wake up this morning, roysh, in Christian's gaff on Ailesbury Road, focking amazing pad, and I am absolutely reeking of, like, toothpaste. Christian comes into the room, roysh, and I'm like, "What the fock is that smell?" He goes, "You must rest. You've had a busy day." I'm like, "Will you quit it with that *Star Wars* bullshit, why am I smelling of toothpaste?" He's, like, all offended. He goes, "I put it on your neck last night. To try to get rid of the..." The whole night suddenly comes, like, rushing back to me. Of course, it had to happen on the one weekend of the year when the sun is, like, splitting the trees and I am focking burning up in the car as I head for Kiely's and, by the sounds of it, roysh, the weather's going to hold for, like, half the focking summer. Some knob on the radio says there's a heatwave on the way, roysh, because the dolphins have, I don't know, come in wearing shades and focking sombreros or something this year. All I can say is that I'm glad I'm heading for the States in June, by which time, of course, the thing will probably be yellow or some focking colour.

I pork the cor around the corner, roysh, take fifty notes out of the old Drinklink and head into the boozer, feeling really, like, self-conscious and wondering whether the thing is, like, visible and shit? I get a pint in and head over to the goys. Zoey and Aoife are sitting with them and they're, like, locked in conversation, which is sort of, like, unusual because they actually hate each other's guts. Aoife asks Zoey why she didn't go out last night and Zoey says she did, roysh, and Aoife goes, "Oh my God, how come you're looking so well." And Zoey says it's Radiant Touch and Aoife goes, "Oh my God, YSL" and Zoey nods and says oh my God it is SUCH a life-saver.

Judging from, like, his body language, though, JP was going to try to be with her, while Oisínn was definitely going to chance his arm with Aoife, or Miss Cacharel as he calls her. JP asks Zoey whether she was in Reynards last night and she says no she was in, like, Lillies and Aoife asks whether it's true that Bono and Matt Damon were in there, roysh, and she says no that was only a rumour and the only famous people in there were two of the news-readers off TV3 and the Carter Twins. Then she says she's going to the toilet, roysh, and when she's gone Aoife says that – oh my God – Zoey looks like shit.

When Zoey comes back from the toilet, roysh, she looks at me and goes, "Oh my God, Ross, what the fock are you wearing?" and everyone looks at me, roysh, we're talking Fionn, JP, Simon, everyone, and I'm wondering whether they know what happened, whether Christian has told them. I presume he hasn't and I just go, "It's a polo-neck. What's the big deal?" Aoife goes, "You do look a bit of a knob in it, Ross". I tell her that polo-necks are in and Zoey thinks for a minute, roysh, and goes, "Oh my God, they are. I read that in *Marie Claire*. They're the new, em, shirts, I think."

I can see Simon sort of, like, sniggering, roysh, and also JP, who I think was actually in Peg's last night, I can't remember, but I'm pretty sure now he knows the story, and all of a sudden, roysh, he tells me that I look like the goy off the Milk Tray ad and everyone storts breaking their shites laughing, roysh, and then Fionn, roysh, he goes, "And all because the lady loves Ross's neck." And Fionn high-fives JP, and JP high-fives Christian, and Simon high-fives...

Well, let's just say that everyone high-fived everyone else.

The Cainty Caincil are warning motorists of severe delays in Stillorgan due to essential raid works but all I know is if this dickhead bus driver thinks I'm letting him out he's got, like, another think coming.

I was never so loaded in all my life, roysh, as I was when me and Oisínn muscled in on the fake ID racket in UCD. The whole of, like, first year was heading to the States for the summer, roysh, and they all needed, like, fake driving licences and shit to get served over there? We were, like, totally up to our tits in work. It was, like, no surprise that I didn't make it into any of my exams, although it was to the dean of our course, who is SO trying to get me focked out of college it's unbelievable. I was like, "Hey, I had things to do. People to see." He went, "I think you need to sit down and re-evaluate whether you're serious about a career in sports management or not." I'm just there, "Get real, will you?"

Fock it, roysh, because I knew I was going to have to repeat anyway and suddenly I had, like, eight hundred bills in my pocket and it was, like money for old rope. A couple of knobs from Ag Science were actually doing it first, roysh, but Oisínn goes up to them in the bor – they were, like, playing Killer – and he goes, "You the goys dealing in the fake IDs?" Oisínn had picked up a focking pool cue at this stage, roysh, and the goys are like, gicking themselves, there going, "What do you mean, fake IDs?" Fionn goes, "Maybe I'm not making myself clear enough. What I'm asking you is whether they're your flyers I saw stuck up in the Orts block?" One of the goys goes, "Where?" And Oisínn, roysh, he plays it totally Kool and the Gang, just goes, "Outside Theatre L." You can see, roysh, that these goys are totally bricking themselves and we're talking totally? The goy goes, "Yeah... Em, they're ours" and Oisínn's there, "Well, what I'm telling you goys now is that there's a couple of new faces on the scene." He points over at me, roysh, and I'm, like, trying to look really hord, but there's no need really because Oisínn is such a big bastard he'd have handled all of those goys on his own if he had to. He goes, "Time to take early retirement, boys. You've enjoyed it while it lasted though, haven't you?" I turn around, roysh, – and I have to say I pretty much surprised myself with this one – I went, "Unless you want to face involuntary liquidation."

So basically that was it, roysh. We put the word around the Orts block that we were the men to see for all your fake ID requirements, then spent most of March and April in the bor, playing pool, knocking back beers and taking orders from people. Fock, I was never so popular in my whole life. Everyone loved us and we're talking totally here. The babes would come in, roysh, and we'd be giving it loads, looking at their passport photographs and going, "You look too well in this picture to put it on a passport" and "You must do modeling, do you?" We're talking The Palace, Annabel's, Mono, I have never seen so much action in my life. We'd get bored snogging one bird, roysh, and the next one was already queueing up behind her.

The goys loved us too. We were, like, celebrities. I'm walking through the library or I'm heading down to 911 for the rolls, roysh, and total strangers are coming up to me and high-fiving me, telling me they're getting the notes together and they'll soon be in touch. And I was like, "Yeah, whatever." Me and Oisínn, for six weeks, we were, like, totally Kool and the Gang. It was not only respect, roysh, there was a bit of fear thrown in as well. Every time he handed over an order, Oisínn goes to the customer, "You breathe our names to the NYPD and you're fish food."

Sometimes, for a laugh, roysh, we'd print the words, "Póg mo thóin" in, like, really official looking writing on the fake driving licences, roysh, underneath the horp. Póg mo thóin is actually Irish for All Cops Are Bastards, which basically completely rips the piss out of them without them actually knowing. Everyone loved that little touch. They were like, 'Oh my God.'

And the work was a piece of piss. Oisínn, who knows a bit about computers, he downloaded this, like, thing off the internet, what he said was a template for a driving licence, and he gave it to me on, like, a disc? So I'd go home, roysh, get onto the old man's computer, add in the customer's name, date of birth and all that shit, print it out, Pritt Stick the photograph onto it and take them down to the video shop where this bird I know called Keeva laminated them for us. We didn't cut Keeva in on any of the profits. Oisínn said it was to protect her, but the real reason was that she didn't want any money. I have to say, roysh, and I'm not being big-headed here, but she did it for love. She's been, like, mad into me for years, ever since transition year actually, when we both did our work experience in her old man's architect's firm. She's actually pretty alright looks-wise, a little bit like Jennifer Love Hewitt from a distance.

So for five weeks, roysh, me and Oisínn, well, we had it all. Money. Babes. Fame. But all good things have to come to an end. As Christian always says, there's always a bigger fish. So this day, roysh, me and Oisínn are sitting in the bor, knocking back a few beers with this goy from second year law, who we brought on the lash for being our five hundredth customer, when all of a sudden, roysh, these five Chinese goys come in and say they want a word. Oisínn plays it totally cool, roysh, going over and sitting down with the goys and talking for, like, five or ten minutes. Then the Chinese goys, like, head off.

Oisínn comes back over, roysh, takes a long swig out of his bottle of Heino and goes, "We're folding the business, Ross." I'm like, "Who were those goys? And why did they all have their little fingers missing?" He goes, "Why do you think, Ross?" I go, "My God, they're not from Newtownmountkennedy, are they?" He shakes his head and goes, "We're not talking genetics here, Ross. These goys are Triads." I'm like, "Triads?" He gets three more beers in and goes, "Yeah, Triads. You don't fock with those goys." I'm there, "It was, like, good while it lasted though, Oisínn, wasn't it?" He just, like, stares off into space, roysh, and eventually he goes, "Involuntary liquidation. I liked that... Have to hand it to you, Ross, you're a stylish bastard."

The radio's going, if you're paying your home insurance to your mortgage company you could be paying too much and all of a sudden this complete asshole in a red Corsa, roysh, he pulls right out in front of me, no indicator, nothing, and I have to hit the brake and drop down to something like third gear or something, roysh, and I am going to be SO late because there's focking raidworks in operation on the Rock Raid and the saithbaind carriageway of the M50 between Scholarstown Raid, and the Balrothery Interchange is still claised, causing severe delays on all approaches to the Spawell randabite and I'm wondering when the FOCK they're actually going to sort out the roads in this country, and all of a sudden we're stopped at lights, roysh, and I get out to have a focking word with the total penis in the red Corsa and he sees me coming and, like, winds down his window and he goes, "I'm really sorry about that" and I'm like, "If you don't know how to drive you should have a focking L plate on your cor".

Sorcha, roysh, she had her 21st, roysh, and it was a big, fock-off, black tie affair in Killiney Golf Club, we're talking free bor, the whole lot. Anyway, roysh, I only found out the night before that my parents were, like, invited as well and I went ballistic. I'm there going, How the fock am I going to score with the old man and the old dear in the same room. I'm like, "You're not actually thinking of going, are you?" The old dear's there, "Mr and Mrs Lalor want us there. They're friends of ours, Ross" and then she's like, "I hope you've bought Sorcha something nice." I go, "What I bought her is my business," which basically means I bought her fock-all, because I totally forgot, what with the exams storting next week and me having to get, like, all the lecture notes off the internet.

So I headed out to Stillorgan that afternoon, roysh, and I ended up getting her a fake Burberry bag in Dunnes, which is a bit scabby I know, but I only had, like, ten bills to spend. I meet the goys in the Druid's Chair for a few scoops beforehand, roysh, and then we head down to the golf club and there's Sorcha's old pair, at the door of the function room, roysh, welcoming everyone as they arrive, and Sorcha's sister, Afric or Orpha or whatever the fock her name is, she's collecting all the presents and making a list of who gave what, which will no doubt be discussed in detail at the Lalor breakfast table tomorrow morning.

I'm, like, standing in the queue behind this bird Becky, roysh, who's, like, second year Commerce in UCD, a little bit like Jaime Pressly when she's wearing her contacts, and she's says she's, like, SO bursting to go to the toilet, roysh, and she asks me to mind her place in the queue for her and, like, her present. A big fock-off present it is as well. So she goes off looking for the jacks, roysh, and I'm standing there with this little scabby present from me and this, like, massive one from Becky and all of a sudden I'm at, like, the top of the queue and Becky still isn't back, so I switch the two cords. Sorcha's old dear air-kisses me, roysh, and looks over her shoulder to some friend of hers, maybe from the ladies golf club, and goes, "This is Ross. He was on the Castlerock team that won the cup." Sorcha's old man shakes my hand, real, like, formal and shit, and then Aifric kisses me on the cheek and then storts, like, giving me the serious eyes, obviously jealous that her sister's getting all the attention tonight and deciding that being with me again would be the best way to piss her off. I hand her the big present, roysh, and I go, "This is from me." She's there, "Oh my God what is it?" I'm like, "Something special".

And she looks at the other present, roysh, the wrapping paper all ripped and she, like, turns her nose up at it. The goys were, like, focking the thing around the place on the way down, practicing their line-outs with it and shit. I'm like, "That one's from Becky. I think she was too embarrassed to give it to you herself." Afric says she doesn't blame her and, as I go to head inside, she tells me I SO have to promise I'll dance with her later.

I get inside, roysh, and even though it's, like, totally jammers in there, the first person I see is Sorcha, who is looking totally amazing in this black dress, roysh, which I overheard Emer say is a copy of the one that Jennifer Lopez wore to the Grammies. I have to say, I've never seen her looking so well. Every goy in the place is, like, hanging out of her, but she comes over to me, roysh, and airkisses me and oh my God she smells focking amazing, possibly Ultra-violet by Paco Rabanne, I'll have to ask Oisínn. She goes, "I didn't know if you were going to come." I'm like, "You look amazing." She goes, "I'm glad you did."

I look into her eyes, roysh, and I'm like, "Did you hear I might be playing for Blackrock next year?" and suddenly she's like, "Don't, Ross." I'm there going, "Jim Leyden invited me down to Stradbrook. To check out the facili-ties." She's like, "You're wasting your time." I'm like, "I'm just telling you I'm thinking of going back playing serious rugby next season." And she goes, "And I'm just telling you that I'm going out with someone, so please don't start any trouble." Off she focking storms, roysh, and 'Stuck In A Moment' comes on and Oisínn comes over and grabs me in a headlock and goes, "She is GAGGING for you tonight, Ross." I'm like, "I know. I told her I'm not inter-ested, but she just can't seem to get her head around it." Fionn goes, "Would anyone with any information on the whereabouts of Sorcha's self-respect, please contact gardai at Shankill."

So we're there for the night, roysh, knocking back the pints and about eleven o'clock, Zoey and Sophie come around telling us all to go and "get food" because there's, like, loads of it there and we can't let it go to waste, which, as Fionn says, is a bit rich coming from, like, Calista Flockhart and Geri focking Halliwell, but we join the queue anyway, roysh, and who's standing right in front of me only the old man and he's chatting away to some complete knob about, I don't know, the federal reserve, whatever the fock that is. He sees me and goes, "Ross, have you met Killian? He's with PriceWaterhouse." The goys goes to shake my hand, roysh, but I just look him up and down and go, "Wow, Sorcha's done REAL well for herself" and I turn around and join in a conversa-tion with JP and Oisínn, who are talking about Formula One.

I'm heading back to where I was sitting with my food, roysh, we're talking lettuce, tomatoes, egg mayonnaise and other shit that doesn't actually go with beer, and I pass the old dear and she's, like, engrossed in this conversation with Sorcha's old dear about Stella McCartney and some place in Greystones which is, like, the only focking shop in Ireland that sells her shit, and they see me as I'm trying to squeeze past and the old dear goes, "Ross, did you meet Killian? Sorcha's new boyfriend? He's with PWC" and I tell her she's a sad bitch.

It's, like, an hour later, roysh, and I look over the far side of the bor and the old man is still there talking to the goy and I feel like going over and asking him whether he, like, still considers me his son at all. Christian is off his face. He keeps reminding me that we've been best friends since we were, like, five years old, roysh, and that I'm a good goy and that's not the drink talking, and I'm the best focking friend any focker could hope for, and even though I turned to the dark side for a little while he always knew there was good in me blah blah blah.

I knock back a vodka and Red Bull that JP bought me and then this bird, Gemma, who's, like, repeating in Bruce, passes by, looking pretty amazing and I can see what the goys mean when they say she looks like Ali Landry, and all of a sudden I look up and Sorcha is, like, standing next to me again. She goes, "She's seeing someone, Ross." I'm like, "Gemma? I wasn't actually..." She's there, "I'm only kidding. She broke up with Ronan ages ago. Do stay away from her, though, and I'm telling you that as a friend. That girl has a serious attitude problem." I nod, roysh, sort of, like, taking what she said to me in, and all of a sudden, roysh, Fionn, like, breezes past us and goes, "Alright Sorcha? How's things in Capeside?" which she doesn't actually hear, although I have to try really hord to stop myself, like, bursting out laughing.

Sorcha goes, "How was the Florida salad? Mum made it. It's, like, a secret family recipe." I go, "Sorcha, you didn't come over here to ask me about Florida salad," pretty confident at this stage that she wants to be with me and she's there, "Well, you're right, Ross. I came over because I wanted to say sorry to you." I'm like, "It's cool." She goes, "I know my saying sorry to you is becoming, like, a ridiculous refrain, but I wanted to apologise for misjudging you, Ross. I've just opened your present." I'm like, "O-kaay," totally bluffing it because obviously I don't have a focking clue what it was I gave her, roysh. She goes, "Those cases are SO expensive, Ross." I'm like, "Ah, it was nothing, Sorcha. Just a little token of my affection." She goes, "Little? HELLO? They were

Louis Vuitton?" I'm like, "Forget about it. By the way, what did Becky get you?" and Sorcha goes, "Do NOT even talk to me about that girl. Anyway, Ross, the reason I was so happy about your present is that you seem to have accepted what's happening." I'm like, "Happening?" She goes, "Well, yeah. You've obviously heard that I'm going to Australia for a year. With Killian? That's why you bought me the case?" I'm like, "Yeah, of course. When are you off?" and she goes, "Next week", and she kisses me on the cheek, roysh, and she tells me she is SO going to miss me. And then she heads off. Christian throws his arm around my shoulder and asks me whether I know how long it is since we've been best friends and I can feel tears in my eyes, roysh, and Christian is, like, serious all of a sudden and he asks me if I'm crying and I say of course I'm not focking crying, it's the focking dry ice in my eyes.

The old man's solicitor recommended that he reach a settlement with the Revenue Commisioners, roysh, so he was going out to Portmarnock to discuss it with him over an early morning round of golf and he asks me to drive him, obviously planning to have a few scoops, and I tell him I will, roysh, because I'm, like, trying to stay on the right side of him, what with me going to the States in a few weeks and needing, like, six or seven hundred notes to bring with me. So there we are driving along, roysh, and the old man's there going, "He wants me to settle for a hundred thousand pounds, Ross. I could buy a land rezoning for that" and I'm, like, seriously fighting the urge to call him a spa and tell him to shut the fock up. Being up at, like, seven o'clock on a Saturday morning is bad enough without having to listen to him bullshitting on.

So anyway, roysh, basically what happened was that I ended up breaking a red light at the bottom of, like, Stradbrook Road and this woman in a red Subaru Signet comes around the corner and, like, ploughs into the side of me. It's a good job I'm driving the old man's Volvo and not my Golf GTI because I would have had a complete eppo. As it turned out, roysh, there was, like, fock-all wrong with the old man's cor, side impact bors, the thing's a focking tank, but the front of this woman's cor was, like, pretty badly damaged and shit. The second it happened, roysh, the old man goes, "Leave the talking to me, Ross. The first line here is all-important." And the two of us get out and walk up to the driver's side of her cor and she, like, winds down the window and the old man goes, "Is your neck alright?" The woman, roysh, she's a total howiya, she's there, "Me neck's grand." And the old man turns around to me and goes, "You heard that. That cuts off any possible spurious claim for whiplash at source" and then he, like, whispers, "Don't get me wrong, Ross, I've nothing against quote-unquote working class people, but hit one of them in a car and two weeks later she's wearing a surgical collar and looking for twenty grand from your insurance company."

Anyway, roysh, the bird in the Subaru Signet, she storts going totally ballistic, roysh, basically accusing me of breaking a red light, which I totally denied, even though I did. The old man, you have to admire him even though he's a total prick, he goes, "Am I to take it from your tone that you intend to claim from my insurance for this accident?" The woman's like, "Fucking right I do." And her daughter, roysh, who's sitting in the passenger seat beside her, big-time skanger, she storts, like, shouting at me as well, telling me she's going to miss her flight to England. I'm there, "Fock off back to Knacker-agua." And the old man, he turns around to me and goes, "Let me handle this, Ross. I haven't kept my insurance premium low for so many years without knowing a trick or two." Then he turns around to the daughter, roysh – we're talking shiny tracksuit and a shit-load of rings all over her fingers, looks like she's focking mugged Doctor Dre – and he asks her what time her flight is at and she says her check-in is at half-seven. The old man looks at his watch and goes, "It's already a quarter past seven, you do know that, don't you?" The daughter, roysh, she goes, "So what?" and the old man's like, "Well, you're late for your flight and were obviously in too much of a hurry to watch the road in front of you." And she just loses the plot then, telling the old man he's this and that, then actually saying the crash happened because I was on my mobile. Basically, roysh, I wasn't on my mobile, but I was checking my messages when I broke the light, though I wasn't going to admit that, not with the old man basically kicking their orses for them.

He goes, "I'm not saying that you were speeding to try to make the flight, but that's how a judge might look at it." She hadn't a focking clue what to say then, the daughter. The mother, roysh, she's like, "A judge?" The old man goes, "Of course. If you think you're sending my premium soaring through the roof for this bucket of bolts, you can think again." Then he's like, "Your daughter's off to England then?" The mother goes, "Yeah, to see her fella." The daughter's like, "Don't tell them nuttin', Ma." The old man goes, "Did you have a send-off for her last night then?" And the mother, roysh, she just, like, shrugs her shoulders and goes, "Just went down the local." The old man's like, "Have a few drinks, did we? A few lagers perhaps?" She goes, "I only had three glasses." He's like, "Did you know you could actually still be over the limit?" The daughter jumps in then. She goes, "Are you saying my ma's locked?" He goes, "I'm not in any position to judge that. I'm going to call the Gardaí. They can breathalyse her." Then he goes, "OR… you can get back in your little banger there and be on your way."

So they think about it for a few seconds, roysh, then they fock off, calling me and the old man every focking name under the sun. The old man storts, like, debating out loud whether he should still call the cops, maybe report them for leaving the scene of an accident, just so they don't have any second thoughts about claiming. In the end he doesn't bother.

I meet Chloë in Hilper's and she asks me whether I went out at the weekend and I tell her I was in Annabel's and she goes OH my God she was in The George and she had the most amazing time and she went with Julian and Kevin, two friends of hers who she says are ACTUALLY gay but they're, like, really, really good friends of hers, and that's the thing about gay people, they're SO easy to talk to and she says that even though she's not, like, gay herself, roysh, going to The George is SUCH a good night out if you're a girl, because you're not, like, getting constantly hassled by goys all night.

Emma says OH MY GOD, she cannot BELIEVE that Joey told Dawson she never slept with Pacey, the girl is SUCH a bitch it's unbelievable and Fionn, who's been sort of, like, seeing her, he throws his eyes up to heaven and asks whether anyone's, like, going to the bor. Emer says that if anyone is would they get her, like, a pint of Budweiser and Sophie shoots her this filthy, roysh, and Emer goes, "You are not going to make me feel guilty about having a pint." Sophie's there, "I'm just wondering what happened to your diet, that's all. You had a latte this morning." Emer's there, "So?" And Sophie goes, "So… that's, like, eight points or something. And a packet of peanut M&Ms." Emer's like, "You are not going to make me feel guilty about having a pint." But when JP brings it over, roysh, she hordly even touches it.

Fionn, roysh, he stands up and goes, "Look at this," and he grabs the waistband of his chinos and, like, pulls it out and there's, like, enough room to fit Sophie and Emer in there. Sophie goes, "Oh my God, that is, like, SO unfair. You eat like a pig." And Emer goes, "How come your trousers are falling off you?" And Fionn's like, "I just moved up from a 34 to a 38", and he, like, cracks his shite laughing, roysh, and high-fives Christian and JP and then goes to high-five me, and when I don't respond, he goes, "Anyone with any information on the whereabouts of Ross's life, would they contact Gardaí at Harcourt Terrace."

JP goes, "Yeah, what's the crack, Ross? You're very quiet." I'm like, "I'm cool. Leave it." Then he goes, "Listen, I've a great idea, goys. I'll ring the old man, see can I take the day off work tomorrow, and we'll go on the serious lash." Christian goes, "Oh my God I knew I should have put a toilet roll in the fridge." JP says he could get us into, like, Lillies, roysh, and Emer says oh my God we will never guess who was in there last Saturday night, we're talking that goy off *Don't Feed The Gondolas*. Emma goes, "Don't forget Niamh Kavanagh." Erika, who's in a snot as usual, says she's not going anywhere if Beibhinn is going to be there and Emer asks what her problem with Beibhinn is, roysh, and Erika says it's basically because she puts on a skanger accent and that whole knacker-chic thing is, like, SO sixth year.

I can't, like, bear this shit any more, roysh, so I tell the goys I'm heading up to the bor, but I don't, I actually just fock off home. Sorcha has been gone for, like, ten days and I actually didn't think I'd miss her so much. Oh my God I actually could have ended up being with Erika in Annabel's last weekend, roysh, she was giving me the serious come-on and we're talking total here, but I couldn't even be orsed trying. She rang me a couple of days before she left, we're talking Sorcha here, told me she was having a going-away just for, like, family and a few really close friends and she asked me to go because she SO wanted to say goodbye to me properly and I told her I wouldn't miss it for the world. In the end I didn't bother my orse even going.

Spent the night at home, basically going through old stuff, looking for the Holy Child scorf she gave me the first night I was with her. We'd beaten Clongowes in the cup, roysh, and her and all her friends came over to me after the game. It's like it was yesterday. We were all, like, 'Here they come, goys, the Whores on the Shore', but she was so, like, sincere. She goes, "Congrats, you'd a great game." Of course, I'm like, "Thanks", playing it totally Kool and the Gang. She goes, "Do you remember me from the Irish debating team?"

I'm like, "Yeah," even though I hadn't a clue. It was, like, on to Annabel's that night and the next thing I remember is waking up the next morning in Christian's gaff with the scorf tied around my waist.

I also went looking for the Valentine's cord she sent me last year, roysh, telling me she would always love me no matter what, but I couldn't find it, though I did find the menu from her debs, the one that she wrote on saying she'd never met a more amazing person than me before and if there was, like, one goy she'd like to spend the rest of her life with, then it would be, like, me. It's funny, roysh, I don't actually remember ripping it in half.

I drive out as for as the Merrion Centre. It's, like, Thursday evening, we're talking late night shopping night. I'm thinking about the night after her 21st, when I called up to her and made a complete spa of myself asking her not to go away and she just, like, put her head in her hands and went, "Ross, I cannot deal with the soap operatic implications of what you're saying right now." I pass by her old dear's boutique and have a sly look in but her old dear's not in there, just some other woman who works for her. I go into the chemists, roysh, and head down the back to the perfume counter and pick up a bottle of Issey Miyake. I spray some on the palm of my hand and stort, like, sniffing it, roysh, and the woman behind the counter goes, "Can I help you, sir?" I just blank her. I spray some on my other hand, roysh, and it's weird because, like, so many memories suddenly come flooding back and your one who works in the shop suddenly comes out from behind the counter, roysh, and goes, "Excuse me, sir, do you know that that's women's perfume you have there?" I'm like, "No shit, Sherlock" and she tells me to leave the shop or she'll, like, call security. I'm there, "I'm going nowhere", but then this big security goy comes in, so I head off, and he tells me he never wants to see me hanging around the shopping centre again, so I head back downstairs to the cor pork and I think about texting Sorcha but, like just about everything else in my life, it's too late, we're talking too focking late.

The old dear asks me whether it was me who broke her John Rocha signature votive, roysh, and I'm like, "Oh my God you are SUCH an asshole. I cannot wait to get to the States."

When we were kids, roysh, Christian's mum and dad brought the two of us to Lansdowne Road to see Ireland play. It was, like, a Five Nations match against, like, Scotland and though I don't actually remember much about the game, roysh, I know we lost by, like, three points or maybe it was six, but we lost anyway. Christian said Ireland were crap and his old man said they were far from crap, that if they had in their limbs what they had in their hearts then they'd win the Grand Slam every time. We waited in our seats until about ten minutes after the final whistle, roysh, then we headed around the back of the West Stand and Christian's old man decided we were going to, like, wait in the car park and cheer every Irish player onto the bus, to let them know that their courage was appreciated by at least some fans.

Me and Christian both had programmes, roysh, and his old man gave us a pen each to get the autographs of the players as they came out. I'm pretty sure it was raining and Christian's old dear put up her umbrella and, like, pulled the two of us under it and I can remember smelling her perfume, roysh, and thinking that she smelt good enough to eat. I always wanted to take a bite out of her. After about an hour, roysh, the players started to come out in twos and threes and, like, make their way to the bus, but I didn't really recognise that many of them, except Brendan Mullin and Donal Lenihan and maybe Willie Anderson. I got loads of autographs, though. Brendan Mullin asked me my name and then he signed it, "To Ross, best wishes, Brendan Mullin", which I remember Christian's old man telling me he didn't have to do. "A great ambassador for his sport and his country," Christian's old man said. "He didn't have to do that, you know?"

Then Brian Smith came out, roysh, and pretty much everyone there wanted to get his autograph because he was, like, a major star at the time, so there was all this, like, pushing and shoving to get at him, roysh, and I ended up falling over in this puddle and I was, like, soaking wet and my knee was all, like, grazed and shit? I was, like, bawling my eyes out, more out of embarrassment than anything else, roysh, and Christian's mother helped me up and told this man who just happened to be standing beside me when I fell that he ought to be ashamed of himself, carrying on like that, and the goy told her he didn't push me, that I fell and Christian's mum just looked at him and shook her head.

I remember she rolled up my trouser leg and she took, like, a piece of tissue out of her pocket and licked it and then used it to clean the blood off my knee. Then she used another piece to wipe my eyes and she, like, gave me a hug and Christian's old man asked us how we'd like a Coke and a packet of crisps and we went to the Berkeley Court, or maybe it was Jury's, it was one or the other, and that's what we had, Coke and crisps, and me and Christian were, like, flicking through our programmes, looking at all the autographs we'd got, trying to make out who they all were, and I had this, like, squiggle that Christian didn't have and his old man asked to see it, roysh, and he told me it wasn't an Irish player at all, it was actually Gavin Hastings and he told me I was a lucky man to get the great Gavin Hastings's autograph.

Went to the Trinity Ball. Wasn't actually going to go, roysh, had pretty much no intention of going, but I ended up getting asked by this bird, Linley, who's from, like, Blackrock, we're talking second year law, pretty decent looking, a little bit like Catherine McCord, though I have to admit not in the old body department. Basically she was going out with this complete asshole who's in Trinity, roysh, I sort of knew him when he was in Terenure, a complete dickhead whose name I can't even remember, but anyway, roysh, it turns out that he did the dirt on her when she was in Germany on Erasmus for a year and she phones me up the night before the ball, roysh, bawling her eyes out and telling me all this and telling me I'd never guess who of all people her so-called boyfriend did the dirt on her with and she tells me it was Shauna the girl who is SUPPOSED to be her best friend. I'm like, "Bummer." To cut a long story short, she goes, "If he thinks I'm staying away from the Trinity Ball, he has another think coming. I'm going to go, Ross, and I'm going to look SO amazing", and then she asks me to go with her. She's like, "Just as friends, Ross", although I'm pretty sure that the second she sees her ex bet into someone else she will be all over me and we're talking all over.

Catching a girl on the rebound is a difficult one because, as Fionn always says, "you never know what angle they're coming at you from." He says this to me the day before. He goes, "Is she just using you as a bargaining chip to renegotiate the terms of her relationship with this dickhead she's been going out with? Or are you actually going to get your bit? It's fifty-fifty, Ross." I have to say, roysh, I've actually faced worse odds than that in my life when it comes to birds, which is why I told Linley I'd go after thinking about it for, like, two seconds.

Only problem was that my tux was, like, completely focked after the B&L ball and we're talking totally here. So I goes into the old man, roysh, and I tell him he's going to have to spot me six-hundred bills and he's there, "What for?" I'm like, "I need a tux." He goes, "Can you not just dry clean the one I bought you for your Debs?" I'm like, "What the fock is this, Twenty Questions? There's vomit on it. It's focking Pernod vomit. It's not going to wash out. Are you satisfied with that explanation?" He's like, "But £600, Ross. I mean, why is it costing that much?" I'm like, "Because that's how much Hugo Boss focking wants for it. Oh my God you are SO wrecking my head. Just give me the money."

I get the money, roysh, and I end up heading into town with Woulfie, this goy I know from UCD, another ex-Nure boy but, like, totally sound? We hit Michael Howard and get the new threads and then it's, like, fast-forward to ten o'clock that night, roysh, and we're in the Pav, completely focking buckled up at the bor and it's, like, me, the Woulfe man, Ed and Barser, these other two goys who were in Castlerock with me, total focking brainboxes the two of them, doing politics or some shit in Trinity, never really into rugby but they're, like, sound as a pound. Their birds are off, I don't know, mingling or something, but Linley is, like, stuck to me like I don't know what, pretty much cramping my style I have to say. The goys are talking about, I don't know, some focking by-election in Tipperary and Linley, oh my God she is such a dizzy bitch, she keeps butting in, going on about how she is SO thinking of joining Amnesty International again and some friend of hers called Lia who has been nagging her about it for ages, but she decided she was so going to get her finger out and do it after hearing about what's going on in Angola. She goes, "Or maybe it was Ecuador." And I can see the goys, roysh, even Woulfie, just looking at me, going, "Yeah, nice bird you've got there, Ross."

Eventually, roysh, we manage to lose her when she goes off to find Shauna for, like, a clear-the-air meeting, and about half an hour later I see them outside the Pav, hugging each other and bawling their eyes out and saying how much they SO don't want to lose each other as friends. Me and the goys, roysh, we end up drinking cans of Scrumpy Jack in a field in the middle of Trinity, which sort of sounds, like, a bit skangery I know, but as Wouflie says, roysh, knacker drinking is acceptable in a certain context.

I ended up borfing my guts up around midnight, roysh, not because I can't, like, hold my drink, but because of all the focking vol-au-vents that Linley's old dear made me eat when I called out to pick her up. She had this whole big date thing going on in her focking head, roysh, even pulls me aside at one stage to tell me how she didn't want to see her daughter get hurt again and how she hoped I was a nice goy. I turn around to her and I'm like, "Get real, will you?"

Anyway, where all this is leading to, roysh, is that towards the end of the night, Woulfie disappears, we all presume to go off and get himself a score, or to find a place to borf, but then Ed and Barser, roysh, they stort totally freaking me out by going on about the IRA and shit. It's, like, the new Provos this and the new Provos that and oh the new Provos having a porty next week. So I sort of, like, make an excuse to leave, roysh, and I go looking for Linley, because I'm pretty much gagging for it at this stage, and I'm looking through all the tents and, like, half an hour later I find her, roysh, and she is all OVER Woulfie. I am not shitting you here, we're talking ALL over.

And her make-up, roysh, it's all over her face, like she's been crying, so I presume she's been wrecking the goy's head for the past two hours about this ex of hers, who's probably already stuck into someone else, but then I notice that the Woulfe man is playing this whole scene Kool and the Gang, giving it, "He doesn't deserve a girl like you", and she is hanging out of him. There's this big mad inflatable swan outside the gates, roysh, and I can hear Linley asking him what it's for, as if he'd focking know, and he goes, "It symbolizes how anyone can grow into a beautiful creature and have a meaningful life." She pulls away and looks at him like he's focking mad or something and she's there, "Everyone?" And he's like, "Well, everyone with money." She's there, "Oh my God I SO want to be with you." And even though I want to deck Woulfie at that moment, even though I so want to deck the focker, I can't. I just have to admit the goy's got class.

# Chapter Five

## The one where Ross peels crabs

Going from Dublin to the States, roysh, is a total culture shock. *Judge Judy* is actually on in the morning over here and you can't get served in a pub without a fake driving licence. One of the other things that USIT don't tell you is what a total no-no JFK junior jokes are in Martha's Vineyard, which is where me, Christian and Fionn headed basically for a bit of a holiday before we hit Ocean City to, like, look for work and shit? What basically happened this night, roysh, was that the three of us were in this boozer – we're talking me, Christian and Fionn – sitting up at the bor, knocking back beers and, like, joking about business, sport and women, as you do. My memory is a bit fuzzy, roysh, but I do remember Fionn telling us he was ready to, what did he call it, further expound on his theory about girls who are into horses, roysh, and he pushes his glasses up on his nose and takes this really long swig out of his beer, the smug bastard that he is, but just as he's about to launch into this big long speech Christian goes, "I have three words that will make mincemeat of any argument you have." And Fionn, or course, he sees this as a challenge and he's there, "What are your three words?" Christian just goes, "Jodhpurs. Riding boots" and Fionn, roysh, he just smiles and goes, "There are those, I suppose. There are those."

All of this is, like, completely irrelevant, roysh. The point is we all ended up completely off our faces, roysh, and all of a sudden all these knobs came into the pub, obviously locals, we're talking three real college jocks and their birds. We've all stopped talking at this stage, roysh, basically too off-our-faces to say anything, so we're just, like, listening into their conversation, which isn't actually very hord given that they're, like, practically shouting? Anyway, roysh, one of them tells this joke, which isn't even focking funny, it's like, "Did you hear about the new Palestinian Minister for Arts and Music?" And the answer's like, "Yasser I Can Boogie", which is a pretty shit joke, even though they think it's focking hilarious and so, actually, does Fionn, the focking weirdo, who's bursting his shite laughing.

I don't know what put that idea in my head, but I wasn't about to be upstaged, roysh, so I walked over to where they were sitting, we're talking the Americans here, and I can see the bouncers already on their way over – as Oisínn always says, they've got, like, a sixth sense for trouble – and I'm standing over the table, completely rat-orsed, spilling Amstel all over one of them, and I'm there, "What did JFK junior miss most about Martha's Vineyard?" And the bouncers had dragged me out of there even before I had a chance to shout, "The runway."

When we arrived in Ocean City, roysh, we went on the total lash for the first three days, and I got up one Saturday afternoon, we're talking in the total horrors here, and somehow managed to write, like, two letters. One was to Oisínn, who isn't actually coming over now until after the repeats, and the other was to the old dear, which sounds sort of gay, I know, but the thing is, roysh, I thought that if I let her know straight away that I was, like, settled in, then she'd leave me the fock alone for the rest of the summer and I wouldn't end up hearing from either her or the old man again until I needed money sent over.

So the letter, roysh, was just like, "Greetings. Having a great time in Ocean City, which is on the east coast of the States. I've had a good look around the place, checked out some of the local history and stuff and found it really interesting. Fionn and Christian are really into it as well. We've been to about twenty museums so far. It really is a beautiful place, much quieter than Martha's Vineyard and Montauk apparently, which suits me because I'm planning to really buckle down and work hard this summer because to be honest with you I'd like to come back with at least a few hundred bills in September. If I'm going to repeat first year, it's not fair that I ask you to pay for it." Then it was like, "Speaking of money, I was wondering was there any chance you could send me some. Not much. Only like four hundred or something, because the rent is due and I have actually been so busy that I haven't even had time to ring dad's friend about that job. Oh, hey, that's four hundred pounds, not dollars. Anyway, I have to go now. We're off to see a, I don't know, a castle this afternoon. Later, Ross."

About, like, four days later, roysh, I get this e-mail from Oisínn, roysh, and it's like, "What the fuck are you on? What castle? You guys must be doing some serious drugs over there. I can't wait to get there," which is when I realised, roysh, that I'd actually put the two letters in the wrong focking envelopes and the old dear, roysh, she got Oisínn's letter which was like, "Yo, you are missing the best focking crack ever over here. You should have seen the state of us last night. Oh my God, three nights on the total rip and I can hardly remember a thing. I couldn't stand. I couldn't even talk, for fock's sake. I arrived here with the eight hundred bills that the old man gave me and I actually haven't got a focking cent left to my name. Spent the lot in the first three nights. Most of it actually on the first night. The beer is amazing. Total rocket fuel. Milwaukee's Best or, as we call it, The Beast. Twelve pints and I was totally shit-faced and ended up in some focking illegal gambling joint with Fionn and Christian, lost about four hundred notes on the blackjack table, then got thrown out by the bouncers for singing 'Castlerock Über Alles', giving it LOADS, roysh, really letting Ocean City know we'd arrived.

"Ended up hitting this nightclub then to drown our sorrows. Off our faces. We're talking totally here. Met these two birds, Barbara and Jenna with a J they said their names were, though they were as shit-faced as we were. They were like, 'So, what do you guys do for a living?' I'm like, 'Christian's an actor, Fionn's a professional footballer and I'm a navy Seal. What about yourselves?' And Jenna with a J goes, 'We're the President's daughters'. Then they broke their shites laughing. I was playing it totally Kool and the Gang, going, 'I love a good sense of humour. It's one of the things I look for in a girl.' Then it was like, I ended up scoring Jenna with a J. Brought her back to the house and... TOUCH-DOWN! Christened the old bed. Fionn ended up being with Barbara and that left Christian like a Toblerone, out on his focking own. Got up the next morning and it was the usual crack, told her it was a mistake, said I didn't remember a thing, blah blah blah. Last thing we want it a couple of cling-ons with us for the whole summer. Anyway, must go. I'm about to get pissed again and hopefully laid. There's a lot of beer out there and it's not going to drink itself. Rock rules, Ross." And I'm refusing to answer the phone, roysh, which is ringing, like, every half hour and I just know it's either the old man or the old dear, roysh, and they're going ballistic. Having a focking knicker fit, I'd say. Probably won't even send me the money now, wait till you see.

Our landlord, roysh, is this goy called Peasey Pee. He's called Peasey Pee because basically he does a lot of shit and, like, PCP just happens to be the shit he does most. I've been told, roysh, on pretty good authority that it's, like, an animal tranquilliser, but that means fock-all to Peasey, who snorts, like, ten or fifteen lines of the shit a day. He's always offering it to us, roysh, but the goy looks totally wasted, as Fionn says a bit like Iggy Pop with a focking coathanger in his mouth and he's not exactly a good advertisement for the shit he's trying to sell.

But Peasey's sound, roysh, and we're talking totally here, because without him we would be so up shit creek it's not funny. We basically arrived in Ocean City with, like, no jobs, nowhere to live, nothing. We had a little bit of money left over after Martha's Vineyard for, like, a hotel for the first few days, but the money soon runs out, especially when you're, like, drinking for Ireland as we've been doing. After four or five nights in the Howard Johnson, roysh, the receptionist hands us the bill for the mini-bar and the three of us ended up having to do a legger without paying.

So there we are, roysh, wandering around Ocean Highway with nowhere to live, place probably crawling with cops looking for us, and all of a sudden we, like, stumble on this agency, which basically finds accommodation for students and we go in, roysh, tell him we're Irish lads, just over, like, looking for work for the summer, blah, blah, blah, and we need somewhere to live. He tells us, roysh, that pretty much all of the accommodation in the town is already gone, that we've left it very late to be, like, arranging anything. I tell him we were in Martha's Vineyard and he goes, "Were you working there?" and I'm like, "Eh, you could say that, yeah", and I just, like, break my shite laughing in the goy's face and Fionn and Christian, roysh, they're, like, cracking their shites laughing as well and they both high-five me, but when we turn around we notice that the goy hasn't got the joke – Americans, I found out, have basically got no sense of humour – and he's in SUCH a snot now, he just tells us that our only hope is this goy, Peasey Pee, who he says can usually be found down on the beach, flying his kite, and then he's like, "Next, please."

At first, me and the goys thought that this whole kite thing was, like, slang for something, but we ended up finding him just as the goy had said, down on the beach trying to control this big fock-off kite in the wind. Turns out, roysh, it's a hobby of his. He's mad into kites. Kites and PCP. He's about, like, fifty, roysh, we're talking grey hair down to his shoulders, big pointy nose and mad eyes which keep, like, darting all over the place. Fionn goes,

"He looks like a focking photo-fit", which he actually does. I just march straight up to him and I'm like, "We need somewhere to stay." He doesn't answer me, roysh, just nods his head and carries on looking up at the kite. Fionn steps forward then and he's like, "We can pay you four hundred dollars a month. We're talking each." And the goys, roysh, he looks at us for the first time and goes, "What kind of fricking shakedown merchants are you?" I turn to Fionn and I'm like, "Leave the negotiations to me, my man" and I'm there, "Okay, we'll pay you five hundred dollars a month each. No more." He goes, "I want three-hundred and fifty dollars a month off each of you. No less, you leprechaun focks."

He basically haggles himself out of a hundred and fifty bucks, roysh, and ever since then it's been, like, more of the same. The dream landlord. He doesn't give a shit, roysh, that the basement where me, Fionn and Christian sleep is knee-deep in beer cans, condoms and dirty clothes and that it smells like the hippo enclosure at the zoo. We only see him, like, a couple of times a week when he comes in to hide drugs in our cistern and then focks off again and whenever you say anything to him, roysh, whether you're telling him that you've accidentally broken another window or just that a letter arrived for him, he always does exactly the same thing, laughs really loud, shakes his head and goes, "You goddam Irish".

We all end up getting jobs in this local steamhouse, roysh, peeling prawns and crabs and life is basically a laugh, except that the whole social side of things is, like, totally hectic, the old buck-a-beer nights really bringing out the pig in me and the rest of the goys. We've been on the piss for seven days running, roysh, basically spending every penny we earn on booze, and I decide this one night, roysh, that I'm going to, like, crash, recharge the old batteries, whatever, because I am seriously in danger of getting the sack if I'm caught sleeping on the job again and we're talking totally here. So there I am, roysh, sitting in, being very good, watching the wrestling, when Christian, who went out for a packet of Oreos four hours earlier, comes back to the gaff locked off his face and tells us he's won two hundred bucks at Kino, this, like, lottery game they have down in Pickles. Me and Fionn crack on that we're really pissed off with him, roysh, and we tell him his tea's out in the kitchen if he wants to lash it in the microwave and we just, like, carry on watching telly. Scotty Too Hotty is lashing Stone Cold Steve Austin out of it. I turn around to Fionn, roysh, and tell him that this one must be rigged and he says I'm being ridiculous and reminds me that Stone Cold never had what you would term great technical ability and was always overrated as a wrestler, principally due to his ubiquity as the WWF's number one poster boy.

Fionn goes, "Style is no substitute for substance, Ross" and he pushes his glasses up on his nose and, like, out of the corner of my eye, roysh, I can see Christian still standing in the doorway, all upset because he thinks we're in a snot with him. He goes, "I was on my way to get the biscuits and one drink just turned another, you know what it's like. Come on, I've brought you back a present" and he's got, like, a shit-load of drink in a bag, Stinger Lager, twenty-four cans for six bucks or something, we're talking total piss here, but fock it, it gets you shit-faced eventually.

So anyway, roysh, me, Fionn, Christian and these four Belvo heads who live upstairs, we all end up tucking into the cans watching the WWF and what happens? Half an hour later and the beer's all gone and Christian's there going, "Don't be a wuss, Ross. You're coming to the boozer". I'm like, "Christian, I am SO not going out tonight." Of course, ten minutes later, roysh, as Stone Cold is talking us through his amazing comeback against Scotty Too Hotty, we're all heading out the door to Ipanema, this club where we spend the whole night knocking back bottles for, like, a dollar a pop and, by the end of the night, the goys are all locked off our faces, totally horrendified, and we end up getting kicked out of the place because two of the Belvo boys – we're talking Codpiece and the Yeti – they end up dancing on one of the tables when Never Forget comes on and, like, giving it loads.

We decide to head back to Pickles then, roysh, but we can't get in because one of the goys on the door cops that Codpiece's ID is fake and, as we're walking off, roysh, basically telling the bouncers what a bunch of dickheads they are over our shoulders, I look at Codpiece's driving licence and it's a real, like, Fisher Price effort, and I'm there, "This is a piece of shit. It's so obviously a fake" and he goes, "You never said that when you sold it to me." What could I say to that? I'm like, "Come on, let's get a tray of the old National Bohemian and hit the seafront", which we basically did, then when all that was finished, we're talking half-five in the morning here, we headed for the 24-hour Laundromat, which is, like, next door to Pickles.

I'm totally in the horrors at this stage, roysh, and I'm there going, "This whole buck-a-beer night thing is bang out of order. I've a good mind to sue that place." And Fionn goes, "I know, it's socially irresponsible to sell drink so cheaply," and then he storts climbing into one of the spin dryers. Everyone in the place is giving us filthies. He's had his eye on Codpiece's long-standing record of 42 rotations for ages now, roysh, and he's decided that tonight's the night it's going to be broken. He goes, "Someone phone Norris McWhirter," whoever the fock he is, then he hands me his glasses and curls up inside the thing, and the Yeti, who is a big hairy bastard as you can guess, he drops four quarters in the slot and the thing storts spinning and Fionn, roysh, he ends up lasting a very brave 34 rotations, which is actually a Castlerock record, before kicking open the door, sliding out and borfing his ring up all over the floor, the walls, Codpiece's docksiders, everything.

"I've laid down a marker," he goes, as I hand him his glasses back and we head off and all of a sudden we realise that it's, like, bright outside. Ocean City is, like, waking up and we're all sobering up and suddenly everyone has gone really quiet, remembering what a shitty job peeling shellfish is when you've got a hangover, no sleep, roysh, and a seriously dodgy stomach. Coming home at that time of the morning, it's a straight choice between heading back to the gaff for an hour's kip or hitting the nearest 7-Eleven for a cup of black coffee and a packet of Max-Alerts. These pills, roysh, long distance lorry drivers can pretty much drive coast to coast with no focking sleep on them, that's according to the Belvo lads. I am seriously hanging, my head is thumping and I feel like I'm going to focking vom any minute. The thought of work is depressing us all and "I've laid down a marker" is actually the last thing any of us says as we trudge with our heads down in the direction of the shop and then on to the steamhouse.

The old man rings up when I'm out at work, roysh, and he leaves this message on the answering machine. This is, like, word-for-word what he said, roysh. Now you tell me whether you think he's losing the focking plot. It's like, "Hi, Ross. If you're in, pick up. If not, well, I was just ringing to find out how you are, tell you we got your, em... letter, I suppose. By the sounds of it, you're, eh... having a good time. Just, you know... be careful... Em... that's what your mother wanted me to say. Condoms and so forth. Em... I posted you some money. And em... That's it really. No other news. Well, one bit of bad news. Your mother's car is going to have to do the NCT. You know her and that Micra, Ross. She loves the thing. She'll be heartbroken if it has to be... Nothing to worry about, I've told her. It's a super little runner.

"No other news really. Just boring old work stuff really. A bit of trouble in the office at the moment. Em... With the staff. Nothing for you to be worrying about, though, Ross. Don't em... Don't be fretting about your old man, I can cope with these things. You keep on, em, you know, enjoying yourself. Okay, I'm not Bill Gates. Not by any stretch of the imagination. But I know how to run my business. That's one thing I do know, Ross. And if I left it to some of the inverted commas experts who work for me, where would the company be today? Nowhere. That's where. Nowhere with a capital n. Give these people a screen break and the next thing you know they want a bloody crèche on every floor of the building.

"Do you remember that management seminar I went to last year, Ross, where you are, in the States? It was New York, I went with Giles, it was entitled, 'Say Pretty Please and Watch Your Profits Soar'. What a bloody waste of money that turned out to be. Giles and his little fads. Five thousand pounds I paid to hear some so-called authority on employer/employee relations talking about the connection between morale and productivity levels. Not that it's the money, you understand, but... It was all a load of bloody nonsense, that's what I'm saying. And I did give it a chance, Ross. Your mother will vouch for that. I stopped referring to the people who work for me as employees and started to call them quote-unquote stakeholders. But you see the problem was that they thought this new name actually entitled them to something, the bastards... I personally had to sack four of these so-called stakeholders when they started campaigning for an extension to the half-hour lunch break, which has been the standard here for years, Ross. For years. Only takes one or two bad apples.

"Anyway, basically, without wanting to bore you, Ross, because I know I can sometimes be a bit, you know, uncool I suppose, but I just wanted to tell you that I've, em... been getting quite a few dirty looks, I suppose you could call them, in the office over the past few days all because I had the coffee machine removed. I don't want to go into the whos, whys and hows of the whole affair, but basically the word has gone round the office that I did this to save the £60 a month that it was costing me to lease the machine, which is rubbish, Ross. And if I find out whoever it was who wrote on the door of the...

"Oh forget that, your mother's absolutely right. Look, I'm not going to go into the wherefores and the whatnots of the situation, Ross, but basically this all started a couple of weeks ago, at Heathrow airport of all places, when I bought a fantastic book for management types called *Are You Being Taken For a Mug?* The author puts forward this theory – and I am basically in agreement with it – that workers need constant reminding of where the demarcation line between them and management lies. Let them see that you appreciate their efforts and they think they're indispensable. Complacency sets in. Next thing you know, you're washing their bloody cars for them.

"So the upshot of reading this book was that the coffee machine had to go. Now, I know what you're thinking and it did cross my mind, too. Surely caffeine improves productivity, acting as it does to increase alertness, enhance sensory perception, overcome fatigue and improve endurance and motor functions. Nice theory, kicker. But, and I have to emphasise the but here, Ross, the chap who wrote this book, he points out that caffeine is basically an addictive drug, which can have a sedative effect when it's taken in excess. You try operating a company and maintaining profit margins when you've got 400 people on the payroll doped off their heads on fresh ground medium roast by mid morning, oh you'd know all about it then, by God you would.

"Didn't need to finish reading, Ross, my mind was made up. Did you know that coffee can cause panic attacks? Panic attacks. I mean we all know about heart disease and peptic ulcers, but panic attacks. And what was the other one, oh yes insomnia, that was the one that really got to me, because this chap who wrote the book – I'm going to send him a letter, the man has changed my life – he claims that these things account for between eight and twelve percent of all cases of absenteeism. This is America mind you, but I'm sure the figures here are...

"Oh wait, that was the other thing I was going to mention, he says that the average American worker spends, what was it, ah yes I've got it here in front of me, I marked a lot of the more interesting points with post-its and had Susan type them up for me, here it is, the average American worker spends 114 minutes of every eight-hour day standing around chatting to other employees at the coffee machine or water cooler. And what he's saying is that this quote-unquote downtime costs American industry approximately £177 billion every year.

"Now even when you factor in whatever benefits there are from the stimulant effect that caffeine has on the central nervous system of your average worker – we're talking increased attentiveness, reduction in fatigue, etcetera, etcetera – you're still talking about £98 billion. Then factor into the equation the health problems caused by caffeine addiction and you're talking about losses in the region of £121 billion per year. Not my words, Ross. Those are the words of Mark B Finnerty, author of *Are You Being Taken For a Mug?*

"Now I'm not suggesting that I've lost anything like that amount of money, but basically if Maureen and Deirdre want to sit around for half the day talking about their husbands' vasectomies and the traffic on the Lucan bypass, then they can bloody well do it at their own expense, not mine. The machine has been gone for the best part of a week now and I hear you, Ross, I hear you, you're wondering what the net effect of it has been, well I'm coming to that now. Basically, I admit, that productivity is down, marginally, though I'm putting this down to the deliberate go-slow that the staff have organised in a fit of pique and which I'm sure will end when the next round of redundancies and wage reviews are announced just before the summer holidays.

"This Finnerty chap who wrote the book – I must ask Susan to get an address or telephone number for him – he says that an initial dip in output is normal, due to the cold turkey effect that the withdrawal of any drug will have. The symptoms, according to the book, are basically lethargy, headaches and depression, but all are temporary and normal service will resume within four to six weeks. My next dilemma, of course, is what to do about the heat in the office. The same chap has written another book which I'm trying to get my hands on about how an overly comfortable working environment can induce feelings of contentment and sluggishness in workers, with a resultant fall-off in efficiency. Says in the blurb I read that cold workplaces tend to keep workers focused and more attentive, which is basically only common sense when you think about it, though I think I'll wait until the quote-unquote brouhaha over the coffee machine dies down before I start turning down the thermostat, bit by bit, every day, while carefully monitoring its effects.

"Anyway, I'm sure you've better things to be doing than listening to your old dad wittering on. A phone call would be nice, though. Your mother would love to hear from you. In fact, em, we both would, em.., me and your mother. We'll be in tonight if you want to, em... you know, call us. Don't worry about the time difference, it's fine. So, em, talk to you soon."

The thing is, roysh, I don't even know how he got the focking number. I certainly didn't give it to him.

❖   ❖   ❖   ❖   ❖

Christian's old dear never actually worked, she was a bit like my old dear, a Lady Who Lunches. Whenever I stayed over in Christian's gaff, roysh, she used to make ice cream. That's what I always remember. She'd put milk and sugar and that smelly creamy milk, Carnation milk or whatever it's called, into the food mixer, and vanilla flavouring and all sorts of other shit, sometimes fruit, then she'd mix it all up. I don't actually remember having a crush on her at the time but I think I must have.

Z... Y... X... We're talking W... V... U... You can forget pretty much every bit of advice they give to, like, students going to the States for the summer, roysh, the only thing you really need to know is how to say the alphabet backwards, that and how to walk in a straight line with your finger on your nose. If the cops stop you with a skinful of drink on you, roysh, and they know you're, like, Irish and shit, they are are SO going to bust you unless you can show you're not, like, wrecked and shit. And Codpiece – aka Martin Codyre – is the undisputed master at it and we are talking total here. I've seen that goy knock back 15 pints of the Beast, roysh, and then do the whole ZXY thing, while walking on a white line in the middle of Ocean Highway with a full pint on his head. All these cors flying by either side of him, beeping and shit. Doesn't spill a drop. Anyway, roysh, the other night he was teaching me how to say the whole thing off by heart.

And this voice goes, "Will you two fags shut the fock up and go to sleep" and it was, like, Gavin, one of the Belvo lads, who was obviously still bulling because I ended up scoring his bird, or his EX bird should I say, Ciara, in Pickles the other night. Oh my God, what a honey, we're talking the image of Katherine Heigl here. But I'll stort from the beginning. Went to work yesterday. Miracle of focking miracles I've been here for three weeks and I'm actually still employed, though only just. Anyway, I'm wrecked as usual, roysh, not having slept for, like, three nights, because it's like porty, porty, porty, and the old body is storting to build up a bit of a tolerance to the old Max-Alerts.

So there I am, roysh, standing over this big barrel of, like, smelly crabs and shit, having the crack with a few of the Haitians who work with me, and this goy who's, like, their leader and shit – Papa Doc they call him – he goes, "You no look so good, Irish. You whiter than white", which is when I tell him about the keg porties we've been having, we're talking five of the focking things in the last, like, seven days and the old pace is, like, storting to get to me, roysh. He just goes: "I give you something for that" and he brings me down to the steamroom, roysh, where he's got, like, twenty-four cans of the Beast stashed away. He goes, "I believe to you Irish this is called hair of dogs." So there's me and Papa Doc, eleven o'clock in the morning, roysh, in the steamroom, knocking back the beers, totally horendified, and the next thing, roysh, he pulls out the biggest focking reefer this side of, I don't know, whatever the capital of Haiti is. I have to say, roysh, I've never been into, like, dope and shit, but this stuff was amazing. I had, like, three puffs off the focking thing and the next thing I know I'm waking up in the middle of the floor and who's standing over me, roysh, only the boss, we're talking Fatty Dunston himself, and he's there going, "You fucking Irish. This is the last year I employ any of you drunken fucks" and he tells me I'm, like, sacked, roysh, and I didn't know where I was at this stage and I looked up at the clock and it was, like, nearly five.

Papa Doc comes over, roysh, and he goes, "Sorry, Irish. Thought I let you sleep. You tired, man. You tired" and I'm like, "Thanks very much. Now I'm, like, unemployed as well." He goes, "Don't worry. Fatty sack me many, many time. You come back tomorrow, he give you your job back, man." I'm there, "Do you think so?" and he shrugs his shoulders and goes, "Who else gonna work in this shithole for six bucks an hour?" which is, like, a good point. I'll probably end up having to spend a week being the trash monkey, which is the job everyone hates, roysh, going through all the rubbish bags to make sure no knives and forks have been thrown out. The job is usually, like, rostered between about ten of us, but anyone caught acting the dick is usually given it.

But anyway, roysh, the upshot of all this was that I decided to go on the lash for the night, so me and Christian headed for Hooters, roysh, and a load of the Gonzaga and Belvo lads are already in there, we're talking Codpiece, Mongo, the Yeti, and Gavin, who was, like, completely trousered. At one stage, roysh, he corners me and storts telling me all about his ex and how he only went out that night because he heard she was doing to be there and how he loves her, even though he blew it by being with her best friend Jemma at the Muckross pre-debs, and she still hasn't forgiven him for it, even though that was, like, last year, but he's convinced she still has strong feelings for him which is why he ended up coming to Ocean City for the summer, even though most of his mates were actually going to Canada, but he wanted to be close to her because he thinks there's still a chance that blah blah blah. I'm there going, HELLO? Get me out of here, and then he storts focking crying, roysh, going, "My head is so wrecked, I focked up my exams and everything." I think he's first year Commerce UCD. He's there, "I've got to go back to Ireland to sit the repeats and just the thought that she might be with someone else while I'm away is, like, killing me."

And while he's saying all this, roysh, I'm looking over my shoulder at this bird who is giving me loads, we're talking serious eyes here. I have to say, I'm not being big-headed or anything, but I actually looked really well. I can hear Gavin and he's like, "Will you look after her when I'm away?" but I'm not really paying any attention to the goy at this stage, I'm just there going, "Course I will. You can trust me", and I'm looking over the knob's shoulder, wondering when he's going to fock off and leave me alone so I can chat up this bird. Eventually, roysh, after crying into my ear for, like, twenty minutes, he goes up to the bor to get a round in, a pint of Heineken for me and fock knows what for him, and just as I'm about to go over and introduce myself to this bird, roysh, she actually comes over and storts chatting to me, which is when I notice that she's Irish. She goes, "Are you a Yankees fan?" I'm like, "Sorry?" and she's like, "Your baseball cap. Are you a Yankees fan?" And I'm there, "Oh that. No, I just liked the cap. I'm not into American football at all. I'm more rugby." She goes, "American football? Oh my God, HELLO? I thought they were a basketball team. I am SO dumb" I'm like, "I don't think you're dumb. In fact I think you're really intelligent. And beautiful." She sort of, like, blushes when I say that, roysh, and then she goes, "How do you know Gavin?" which is when I eventually cop, roysh, that this is the bird that the dickhead's spent the last three hours crying into my ear about. I'm like, "I don't know the goy. We're just living in the same house." She goes, "The goy is like a limpet."

I go, "I didn't know you were actually Irish until I started talking to you." And she's there, "Oh? Where did you think I was from?" and I don't have a focking clue what to say next, roysh, what country would, like, sound good, so I just go, "Who cares where you're from, as long as you're here now", and she must think this is good, roysh, because the next thing I know she's making a move on me and I have to say, roysh, she's an amazing kisser, and I can understand why this Gavin goy is trying to get back in there. I can also understand why he storts going ballistic when he arrives back from the bor with the drinks, roysh, and catches me and her wearing the face off each other. All of a sudden I open my eyes and the goy's just standing over us screaming the place down and we're talking totally here. He's there going, "I trusted you, Ross. And this is how you repay me?" and he's about the throw a pint over me, roysh, when Christian arrives over, grabs him in a headlock and drags him out of the place, going, "Strong is the dark side, Gavin. Seduce you it can." I ask Ciara for her number and she gives it to me.

Christian has the total hots for this Chinese bird who works at 7-Eleven, roysh, we're talking the one on Ocean Highway here. Pretty much every night he goes in there on his way home from work for, like, M&Ms or Peppermint Patties or whatever we're having for dinner, and he storts, like, chatting her up, giving it loads with the old, "I feel a disturbance in The Force which I've not felt for a long time." And even though most girls think he's actually a complete and utter weirdo, roysh, this bird thinks he's, like, the funniest goy she's ever met. Or she did. Until two weekends ago, roysh, when he decides to go into the shop totally shit-faced, with a traffic cone on his head and his schlong in his hand, and ask her to the Comm Ball. Her old dear went totally ballistic; focked a pricegun at him. It was really, really funny at the time, roysh, but of course we're all, like, borred from the shop now? And considering it's the only place around here that sells the old Max-Alerts, that's a problem, a major problem. We're like, oh my God how are we going to porty AND work?

Christian's reaction, roysh, when I put this question to him the next morning was, "Don't centre on your anxieties, Obi Wan. Keep your concentration here and now, where it belongs." He's focking useless. Me and a couple of the Belvo goys – we're talking Codpiece and the Yeti – we sit down to discuss it, roysh, and between the three of us we decide the only answer is to, like, break into the shop and steal enough tablets to keep us going for the rest of the summer. We'd, like, climb up onto the roof, roysh, smash the skylight, and one of us would be winched down into the shop on a rope. At first, roysh, when the Yeti suggested it, we were all like, 'HELLO?', but as the night wore on, and we were drinking seriously fast, it became, like, the best idea that any of us had ever heard. At, like, three o'clock in the morning, roysh, Peasey Pee calls around to hide more shit in our cistern and we ask him whether he has any rope, roysh, but he just, like, shakes his head, chuckles to himself and goes, "You crazy, cattle-rustling Irish." A few minutes later, he comes back with a huge length of rope, which is, like, four inches thick.

So there we are, roysh, half-two in the morning, we're talking me, Christian, Mad Mal, Codpiece and the Yeti, all wearing our black 501s and our All

Blacks jerseys with the collars turned in, and we're climbing up onto the roof of the shop. It would NOT be an exaggeration to say that I was totally kacking it at that stage and I turned around to Christian, roysh, and I'm like, "If my old man finds out about this, I am history" and he goes, surprise surprise, "Be mindful of the future, but not at the expense of the moment." So we're up on the roof, tip-toeing around on the slates, and I'm just about to ask how we're actually going to smash the skylight, roysh, when the Yeti just puts one of his size fourteens straight through the thing and, after we all tell him what a complete focking dickhead he is, we all stort lowering Mad Mal, who's, like, the smallest one there, down into the shop.

But the second he hits the floor, roysh, the alorm goes off, though fair play to the goy, roysh, he doesn't panic and uses the map that Christian drew for him to find the right shelf and storts throwing packets of pills up through the skylight to us and we stort, like, stuffing them into our pockets. Codpiece had worked out beforehand that we had, like, 200 seconds to do the job before the cops arrived, though this wasn't based on any reconnaissance work he'd done on local police response times but rather the way it always was in the movies. His words, not mine. So Mad Mal's down there, like, three minutes, roysh, and we're all, like, telling him to hurry the fock up, but he goes, "Wait, I just want to grab a few magazines." We're there, "What do you want magazines for?" and he looks up, roysh, his face all blacked up with shoe polish which he's obviously taken from one of the shelves, and he goes, "For the long, lonely nights." The Yeti goes, "Good one, Mal, see have they got Hustler" but of course we should have known better, when we pull the little focker back up, he's got, like, three WWF magazines and we're all there going, HELLO?

Anyway, roysh, we manage to get back to the house before the cops arrive, and we emptied all the tablets into a big bowl on the kitchen table and, like, burnt all the packets in the garden. So that was grand, roysh. Had a couple more cans, ended up going to bed at five, set the alarm for seven to get up for work. We'd only been asleep for, like, half an hour, roysh, when there's all this, like, hammering on the door, and I look out the window and there's, like, a cop car outside and I'm there, "FOCK, IT'S A BUST, GOYS." I wake all the other goys, roysh, and we're all standing there in the sitting-room totally bricking it and the banging storts getting louder and, like, it's obvious that someone's trying to boot the focking door down.

We manage to convince Codpiece to go and answer it, roysh. We're there,

"Just play it Kool and the Gang", so he goes and opens the door, and he's still totally jarred at this stage, roysh, so what does he say? At the top of his voice, he goes, "WE'VE GOT FOCKING RIGHTS! YOU CAN'T SEARCH THIS PLACE WITHOUT A WARRANT!" We heard this, roysh, and we decided there was nothing else we could do except eat the evidence and suddenly we're all there, like, shovelling the pills into us. We must have had, like, twenty or thirty each, roysh, when all of a sudden we heard the goy at the door go, "How many times do I have to tell you, I'm not a fricking cop. I'm a friend of Peasey." And it turns out he was, like, telling the truth. The goy said his name was Starsky, so-called because of his love of, like, cop cars and the one parked outside, roysh, he stole from outside a cop shop in Salisbury, the chicken capital of the world he kept calling it. He said he needed shit, roysh, and he asked whether Peasey had left anything for him and when we said no he goes, "Always the fucking same, that goddam long-hair…" and he focks off.

Of course we're in the horrors now, having just, like, overdosed on Max-Alerts and we are talking total here. Four nights later, roysh, we're all still totally hyper, you know that feeling, you're, like, totally wrecked but you still can't sleep a wink? We're actually sitting in front of the telly a few days later, roysh, we're talking half-five in the morning here, and I'm there, "I feel like I've had seven Es." Of course Fionn, roysh, funny bastard that he is, he goes, "Seven Es? That's what you got in your Leaving, wasn't it?" I'm like, "You are SUCH a dickhead."

The next night, roysh, we still haven't come down so the whole lot of us decide to head for the hospital, we're talking the casualty department here, because it's getting, like, majorly scary at this stage. So we get a taxi down there, roysh, fifteen dollars it cost us, and we all just, like, burst into the place and I grab one of the doctors, roysh, and I go, "We've taken about twenty Max-Alerts each and we haven't slept for days." And he looks at me, roysh, like I've got two heads or something, and goes, "Sorry, we're not recruiting staff at the moment."

I've made a bit of a habit, roysh, of trying to get home from work in the evenings before the rest of the goys, just so I can get to the answering machine first and make sure my dickhead of an old man hasn't left any embarrassing messages. Here, word for word, roysh, is the message he left this afternoon.

"Hey, kicker, guess what...? Oh by the way, pick up if you're in... Hello...? Hello...? Pick up if you're in, Ross... Oh, never mind. Promised I'd keep you abreast of developments vis-à-vis the withdrawal of the coffee machine from the office and any improvements or otherwise in the staff's workrate pertaining therefrom. Nothing to report, I'm afraid to say, Ross, or rather nothing positive. What I can tell you is that in a fit of what I can only describe as pique, with a capital p as well, Maureen, that lippy little madam from accounts, went out yesterday and bought a kettle and four large drums of Nescafé Gold Blend. They were sitting there, Ross, on the draining board in the canteen, brazen as you like, when I passed by there on Tuesday morning.

"All the girls from accounts were in there too, sipping their coffees without a by-your-leave, wittering away among themselves, house prices in Tallaght and Deirdre's going-away party. I'm paying for all of this of course. And you know me, Ross, I'm not what you would call a quote-unquote vindictive man, but I don't mind telling you I headed straight for the petty cash tin to see if these drums of coffee had been paid for from company funds. A sacking offence. Sacking with a capital s, but of course Maureen's much too clever for that. Don't mind admitting the resolve was tested, Ross. The resolve was tested.

"Went home and couldn't sleep. Had a couple of brandies but it was no good. Your mother tried to help, of course. She's a rock, your mother. Just give them their machine back and be done with it, that was her advice. Just trying to be helpful, of course, but that'd be a climbdown I told her. They see one sign of weakness in me and we'll have all that minimum wage nonsense all over again. Wouldn't be a climbdown she said. You don't have to say anything. Just put it back. And then she said something that got me thinking. It got me thinking too much if the truth be told. She said, Charles, I'm sure it takes longer to make a cup of this, what did you call it, instant coffee, than it does to make a cup of the real stuff. And that was me awake for the night. Couldn't get this blasted conundrum out of my head. Which takes longer to make, instant or machine coffee? Couldn't let it go. I had to know.

"By the way, Ross, if you're in pick up, it's unfair to leave me talking into a... Where was I? Oh yes, which is quicker? Well, I remembered that a few months earlier I chanced upon a couple of girls from the marketing department lounging around in the canteen, middle of the morning, drinking coffee, without a care in the world. So I asked them what they thought they were up to. Screen break, they said. Screen break, if you please. Quote-unquote. So

I asked Susan to launch a bit of an investigation, you know how she likes all that cloak and dagger stuff, to find out how long it actually takes to make a cup of coffee, using the machine you understand.

"So, my curiosity pricked by your mother's earlier statement, I remembered that I had a copy of Susan's report in my study. Sleep was out of the question at that stage, so I went and ferreted the thing out. Made for very interesting reading. Very interesting reading with a capital v, i and... She estimated the time it took to brew the coffee first thing in the morning at eight minutes. Each cup made thereafter took approximately 36 seconds, adding five seconds for milk and seven seconds for each sachet of sugar used.

"Armed with this information, I decided to head straight for the office. My pulse was racing, Ross, I don't mind admitting that to you. I looked at the clock. It was four in the morning. The traffic wouldn't be bad for another half an hour yet. Made town in good time, parking the car on Stephen's Green and then letting myself in. Headed for the kitchen. Looked around. No-one else in. Checked my watch. Waited for the second hand to reach twelve, then filled the kettle. Switched it on. And then as coolly as you like – or as coolly as my shaking hands would permit – I started to make a cup of this instant stuff, just as I'd seen it done once. Tried to remember the process as best I could. One-and-a-half teaspoons of cofffee. A drop of milk. Two sachets of sugar. Add the hot water. Stir it until the granules dissolve.

"Oh, well. Instant coffee, my eye. Took almost twice as long to make as the other stuff. From the machine. I went back home then, considering my findings in the car on the way, though in the end I decided to sleep on it and, well, it was such a stressful night I conked out as soon as my head hit the pillow anyway. Still didn't know what I planned do when I went back in the next morning. Then when I got back into the office, who was there only two scruffy looking chaps with long hair, absolutely stinking they were, sandals and God knows whatever else, hanging around the reception area. 'Don't worry,' I told Una, our telephone girl, 'I'll handle this' and then I turned to them and said: 'There are bloody good support services out there for people like you. You'll not be getting a penny from me. Now leave before I call the Gardaí.' You'll never guess what happened next, Ross. 'You don't understand,' one of them said. 'We're from SIPTU. We're here for a meeting.'

"You could have knocked me down with a feather. Maureen had only dragged one of these wretched trades unions into the whole thing. And, well, that's what's really bothering me, Ross. Don't want them hanging around.

Could spell trouble with a capital t. There's been a lot of changes in employment legislation in recent years that I haven't really kept abreast of. But that's it. The gloves are off now. I'm not giving in to the unions. It'll be breast-feeding stations and gluten-free bread for the world and his mother next, wait and see. Better go, think my next move through. Oh, by the way, ring your mother, will you? You know she worries."

# Chapter Six

The one where Ross is in big shit

YOU'RE NOT THE AMERICAN BAD ASS. YOU'RE THE AMERICAN DUMB ASS. RUNNING YOUR MOUTH OFF. A CHAIR TO THE HEAD WILL SHUT YOU UP EVERY TIME. The Yeti is standing on the table as he shouts this and I am SO not in the mood for this shit tonight, especially after spending the last two weeks as the focking trash monkey, I'm sick and I'm tired and I smell like the Blackrock College dorms. The Yeti – I actually don't even know that focker's real name – he's come back from Ipanema totally twisted and we're talking total here. He's wearing a black, sleeveless T-shirt with 'Big Nasty Bastard' on it, roysh, and he's like, "SEVEN FOOT TWO INCHES. FIVE HUNDRED POUNDS. THE BALANCE OF POWER HAS SHIFTED IN THE WORLD WRESTLING FEDERATION. AND TONIGHT, ROAD DOG... YOU ARE MY TARGET FOR DESTRUCTION."

He points at Codpiece, who's completely twisted as well and is at this precise moment in time fixing himself a Bonjela gum ointment sandwich ("Nothing worse than dry bread"). The Yeti jumps two-footed off the table and, like, tries to drop-kick him, roysh, but Codpiece sees him coming and moves out of the way, roysh, and the Yeti hits the sink instead and there's this, like, crash and the whole unit just, like, collapses. Codpiece puts his sandwich down, roysh, and then he starts, like, stamping on the Yeti's neck, and then he drags him to his feet and, like, throws him against the wall. The Yeti comes staggering back towards him and Codpiece clotheslines the focker and he goes, "THE ARM BONE CONNECTS TO THE CHEEKBONE... AND THAT'S THE LIGHTS OUT BONE!"

There is no way any of us is going to get any, like, sleep tonight. The Yeti, roysh, he, like, struggles to his feet, roysh, and goes, "I'VE ALREADY

114

KNOCKED THE UNDERTAKER OUT OF ACTION. I'VE ALREADY KNOCKED THE ROCK OUT OF ACTION. NOW COME OVER HERE AND FEEL THE POWER OF MY ARMS. " And then he hits him, we're talking, like, full in the face here, and Codpiece all of a sudden hits the deck and the Yeti tries to smash a chair over his back, but the thing won't break and he gives up after, like, six or seven attempts. Then I hear this, "Ross, get out of the way", and I turn around, roysh, and it's Mad Mal from Monaghan, who's, like, recording the whole thing on this video camera and he storts doing, like, a running commentary alongside it. He's there, "The Big Show will do to the Road Dog exactly what he did to Scotty Too Hotty... YEAH, WHAT'S THAT?" He's, like, doing the two voices. "YEAH, WHAT'S THAT?... He'll step on his foot and black his eye and when he's done he'll give him a dance lesson... GET REAL. ROAD DOG'S NO SCOTTY TOO HOTTY. HE DOESN'T BLEACH HIS CISSY HAIR. TAKE A REALITY PILL, MAN... Hey, change your attitude, marshmallow head."

Anyway, roysh, Codpiece is back on his feet now and he just, like, grabs the Yeti in a headlock and smashes his head into the wall and – Oh MY God – his head goes right the way through the focking plaster. It's, like, stuck in the cavity and Codpiece is, like, kicking him in the orse and I have to say, roysh, this is actually very funny. Then he gets a chair and, like, cracks it across the back of his legs and this one does break and the Yeti just, like, collapses on the floor and shit.

Codpiece picks up his sandwich and he turns to me and goes, "Ah, Ross, you're home. Are the other goys in?" I'm like, "Don't know. Why?" He takes a bite out of his sandwich and shrugs his shoulders and then he's there, "Thinking about getting together a six-person tag team match with NO DISQUALI-FICATIONS" and I actually don't have time to shout 'LOOK OUT BEHIND YOU' before the Yeti appears from nowhere and cracks him across the back of the head with the kettle and Codpiece is out of it this time, we are talking totally out of it, and the Yeti goes, "LIGHTS OUT!" and then he turns to Mad Mal then and he's, "Did you get that bit on tape?"

Next thing, roysh, the door swings open and it's, like, the landlord and we're like, 'Oh shit. We are SO dead.' He has a look around the kitchen, roysh, which is totally wrecked, the sink's in ribbons, there's, like, holes in the wall, broken chairs, we're talking beer cans all over the place and Codpiece in a ball at his feet. I'm there, "Peasey, we'll pay for any..." and he's there, "SILENCE." We are cacking it at this stage, although I have to say I don't think he'd be stupid enough to call the feds, especially considering the amount of shit he's got hidden in our toilet. Peasey all of a sudden goes, "SILENCE, I SAID... FINALLY THE ROCK HAS COME BACK" and Mad Mal's there going, "ROCKY! ROCKY! ROCKY!" Peasey grabs the Yeti by the scruff of the neck, roysh, hits him in the face with, like, the top of his arm and then throws him across the kitchen. The Yeti hits the back door, roysh, and it comes completely off its hinges and he ends up in the back garden. Mad Mal's going: "That'll leave a mark... I'LL BE VERY INTERESTED TO HEAR WHAT COMMISSIONER FOLEY HAS TO SAY ABOUT THAT ILLEGAL MOVE... Illegal move? Listen, goofball, this guy is the greatest technical wrestler ever to set foot in a ring... THE GUY GOT LUCKY... Lucky? Give me a break... THE KIND OF BREAK THAT ROAD DOG WILL GIVE THE SO-CALLED ROCK IN THE REMATCH?... There isn't going to be a rematch... BECAUSE THE ROCK'S YELLOW, RIGHT?... Wrong. Because the Road Dog is finished business... FINISHED BUSINESS? PA-LEASE..."

Peasey Pee points at me and goes: "I'm kicking your candy ass next, Chris Benoit", and then he, like, opens the door and focks off again and Mad Mal's there, "He's certainly sowing the seeds of dissention there... PROBABLY FOR THE FIRST TIME TONIGHT WE'RE IN AGREEMENT. THIS COULD BE THE FIGHT THAT REALLY LIGHTS UP WWF SMACKDOWN."

I go and check on the goys, roysh, and they're both, like, totally out of it. Codpiece is lying on the floor, head completely in bits, blood all over the place and the Yeti is actually lying on his back in the garden, unconscious, and making these, like, gurgling noises. I leg it down to the end of the street, roysh, to phone an ambulance – we can only take incoming calls – and it arrives, like, ten minutes later and me and Mad Mal hitch a lift to the hospital in the back of it. When we get there, roysh, I tell the nurses in the accident and emergency ward that they were, like, beaten up by a bunch of druggies, which, considering Peasey Pee's record and the fact that he's operating a crack kitchen out of our focking toilet, isn't actually a lie.

So anyway, roysh, they keep the goys in for a few hours and Codpiece wakes up first and goes, "Where the FOCK are we?" and I have to go, "Hospital" and he's there, "What happened?" I go, "You played Smackdown with the Yeti." He goes, "I know, I know. I remember that. But who called the ambulance?" I'm like, "I did" and he's there, "WHAT THE FOCK DID YOU DO THAT FOR?" I'm like, "Because you were unconscious." He goes, "THIS IS GONNA COST ABOUT 800 BUCKS." And then he's like, "Ross, I appreciate your concern for me. In future, basic first aid. Check for a pulse. If you can't find one, then it's time to call the ambulance." Which is when this nurse arrived in, roysh, really good-looking, a bit like Alyssa Milano, or what Alyssa Milano would have looked like five years ago, and she goes, "Do you guys have medical insurance?" And Codpiece, roysh, who's holding a bandage up to this, like, really deep cut under his eye and who looks like he's really shitting it at this stage, he goes, "Now, we don't." And the nurse, roysh, she's there, "How will you be paying for your treatment?" And suddenly, roysh, the Yeti, who's been lying unconscious on the trolley in the corridor for the last, like, half an hour, he jumps up and goes, "I'M COMING AFTER YOU, RIKISHI. YOU ARE MY TARGET FOR DESTRUCTION" and I think I'm basically the only one who realises how much, like, shit we're actually in, and I have to turn to Mad Mal and tell him to turn the video camera off.

I tell Christian that there was a message from his old man on the answering machine when I came home and he goes, "And this affects me how?"

There's, like, fifteen goys staying in our gaff, roysh, or sixteen if you count Blair, which we never really do because he's always so out of it, a total pisshead. Out of the six weeks he's been here, roysh, I'd say he's spent, like, four of them lying unconscious on the floor of the kitchen, which is how he got the nickname Lino Blair. I thought he was dead the other night when I came home from work, stinking of fish, and went to grab a can of beer out of the fridge, which he was lying in front of. I tried to, like, wake him and shit, but I couldn't and I ended up just pulling the door open and whacking it off the side of his head, and even that didn't wake him. The second he heard the ring-pull go, though, he goes, "Ross, you stole my place on the Leinster schools team two years ago. You steal one of my cans and I'm beating the shit out of you", and I'm just there, "Hey chill out, Clongowes boy. This is my beer I'm drinking." He was, like, so lucky he was lying on the ground, because if he hadn't been I'd have decked the focker.

Anyway, roysh, I was far too busy for his shit because I had this bird, Jenni with an i, coming round, second year B&L in UCD, chambermaiding in some focking hotel or other for the summer, a stunner if ever there was one, so like Jessica Alba except better looking if that's possible. She's also doing waitressing three nights a week in Secrets, which is where me and the goys first saw her, though the rest of the lads are, like, totally bulling that I was the one who got in there first.

I went out for a drink with her once, roysh, then invited her around to our gaff to have a drink, listen to a few sounds and whatever, totally forgetting of course that our gaff is a complete shithole. We're talking cans, condoms, cigarette butts and squashed mince pies all over the place and a pool of beer one inch thick covering the whole floor of the kitchen, but of course by the time I thought of this I'd already asked her round, roysh, and it was far too late to try to clean the place up because, as Fionn says, the only way of actually tidying up our gaff at this stage would be to stick thirty or forty pounds of explosives in it and blow the place up.

I ended up borrowing a brush from work, roysh, and sweeping most of the, like, debris, out of the sitting-room, my plan being to try to contain her to just the one room and hoping against hope that she wouldn't notice the smell. Of course the first thing she says when I show her into the sitting-room is, "Oh my God, what is that smell?", and I just go, "Oh, it's something I was cooking" and she looks at me sort of, like, searchingly, I suppose you'd call it, like she was wondering whether I was some kind of Jeffrey Dahmer freak. She storted to relax, though, when I lashed on the old *Pretty Woman* soundtrack, me slyly fast-forwarding it to the end of 'Real Wild Child' and then, halfway through 'Fallen', giving her the old "I've never felt so close to anyone in my life" bullshit, as we both tried to get comfortable on the futon. She says oh my God that song is, like, one of her favourite songs of all time, roysh, but after that the vibes aren't good and by the end of 'Show Me Your Soul', we're talking two songs later, I'm still not getting anywhere.

Basically, it turns out, roysh, that she has a boyfriend back home, some knob called Ryan, who's, like, second year Social Science in UCD and who, she tells me, is working in Cape Cod for the summer, as if I actually GIVE a shit. She ends up boring the ear off me for, like, half the night about this dickhead, it's like, "Oh he's SUCH a good sailor, even I feel safe on the water with him and I can't swim" and it's "Oh he's so romantic, you should have seen what he did for my eighteenth", which is when I finally copped it, roysh. She wasn't giving me bad vibes at all. Basically she was trying to convince herself that she wasn't going to do the dirt with me, even though she knew deep down that she was. I can't believe it took me so long to cop this.

So there I am, roysh, deciding to change my approach all of a sudden, and I'm there, "What's he doing in Cape Cod, this Richard goy?" She goes, "You mean Ryan. He's working. His best friend's uncle owns a country club." I raise my eyebrows and go, "And you're in Ocean City?" She goes, "We just decided to take a break from each other. For the summer like. We're going to New York afterwards for a holiday. Oh my God I am SO looking forward to seeing him again." I'm like, "And do you think he's being faithful?" and she goes, "Of course he is", though she sounded as though she didn't actually believe it as I headed out to the kitchen to grab another couple of cans. Lino Blair was still on the floor but at the other end of the kitchen.

I go back into the sitting-room, crack open the beers and she storts asking me about my exes, some of whom she actually knows. Then we stort having this whole, like, discussion about, like, relationships and shit? That's when I decide to make my move. I'm like, "Do you love him?" She's there, "Who?" and I'm like, "What's-his-name, your boyfriend?" She hums and haws for ages, roysh, bullshitting on about how you can ever really know whether someone is the right person for you and she knows that now especially after what happened with Andrew, blah blah blah, and at the end of this, roysh, she goes, "I suppose I do love him, but I'm not *in* love with him, if you know what I mean."

I know what she means alright. We're talking green light for go here and it came not a moment too soon, because at that stage, roysh, the futon was seriously storting to hurt my orse and I remembered that someone told me, might have been Fionn, that futon is actually the Japanese word for torture, and then I'm like, "All I know is, Joanne" – I actually called her Joanne, though she didn't cop it – "all I know is, if you were my girlfriend I wouldn't want to be away from you all summer." The next thing I know, roysh, she's grabbing my baseball cap off and we're, like, playing tonsil hockey, snogging the face off each other for, like, twenty minutes, roysh, when all of a sudden she jumps up and says she has to use, like, the bathroom? I'm just there going, 'I bet you do'. We're talking five minutes of agonising in front of mirror about whether this Ryan dickhead is doing the dirt as well, a quick blast of Issey Miyake behind each ear and then it's me and her getting jiggy on the floor.

I nip into Christian's room, roysh, just to check whether he's any, like, condoms, and he's already in bed, though he's still awake, and he goes, "Can you two keep it down, you're making me sick." I'm like, "She is SO gagging for me it's unbelievable." He goes, "Come on, Ross, she's an edge of the bed virgin, I can see that a mile off. She'll end up just wanting to talk all night. You might as well kick her out now." I'm there, "You're wrong. I asked her whether she loved her boyfriend and she said yes, but she wasn't actually *in* love with him." He goes, "Shit the bed, you are in then" and I'm like, "I know, that's why I need condoms." He goes, "Ross, I don't have any. We used them all last week. At the keg porty. Remember the water fights?" I'm like "Oh yeah, some focking porty, wasn't it? But what the fock am I going to do now?" He goes, "You'll just have to get off at Sydney Parade." I'm like, "No way, Christian. Please. You must have a secret stash. Come on, I'll owe you big time for this." He thinks for a bit, roysh, then sits up in the bed and goes, "Okay, there's a six pack in my grey Diesel jeans. They're on the back of the chair." I'm like, "Thank you SO much. I owe you for this big-time." He goes, "Yes, young padwan".

Then, roysh, I'm heading back out into the hall when suddenly I hear all this, like, screaming and shit? And then the next thing Jenni with an i comes legging it out of the bathroom, we're talking having a major knicker fit here, bawling her eyes out and everything. I'm like, "Calm down, calm down. What's wrong?" and she goes "The bath, oh my God, it is SO disgusting." I'm there, "It's only Mad Mal's home brew." Mad Mal – or Mad Mal from Monaghan – is this Clongowes border who lives in the house, a total spacer. I'm like, "It's only Mad Mal's home brew. We didn't have a container big enough to make it in."

She goes, "I'm going. Get me a taxi now" so I had to, like, phone the local cab firm, roysh, she was, like, totally hysterical, and she didn't speak a word to me while we waited for it to arrive. I just, like, sat there cursing myself for not keeping her in the one room and then the cab arrived and I knew not to bother, like, asking her whether I could see her again. She just goes, "Well, this was certainly a night to remember", and she gets in the back and then, like, slams the door shut and shit. I went back inside when she'd gone, roysh, tore open all the condoms and left the, like, silver wrappers on the floor beside the futon, basically for the goys to see in the morning, even though I know it makes me a bit of a sad bastard. Then I went into the toilet to flush the unused condoms down the pan, roysh, which is when I noticed this big fock-off rat swimming around in Mad Mal's home brew and that's when I decided that we seriously needed to clean the gaff up.

We get in from A.T.Lantics at, like, four o'clock in the morning, roysh, we're talking me, Fionn, Macker and Oisínn, who's just arrived over, and we're completely off our faces and all of a sudden Fionn notices that there's, like, a message on the answering machine and before I can stop him, roysh, he presses the button and all I can hear is that focking dickhead's voice: "Panic stations, Ross. Your mother's chairpersonship of the residents association is under threat. Stabbed in the back by her quote-unquote best friend. There's no need for you to come home, though. We can handle things here. Just about."

The goys are all breaking their shites laughing. I go to pull the plug out of the wall but Oisínn stops me. "She phoned me at lunchtime today. In hysterics basically. A motion of no-confidence in her leadership has been tabled for tonight's meeting. I left the golf course immediately. Begged her not to do anything stupid before I got home. She was in the study when I arrived, typing out her letter of resignation, tears in her eyes. 'Don't try to stop me,' she said. 'Of all the people who could have stabbed me in the back, why did it have to be Delma?' I have to be strong for her, of course, but I was absolutely fuming inside, because if Delma had been planning this for a while, which she obviously had been, then it stands to reason that Jeff must have known about it too. Yet there he was, at the rugby club annual dinner last weekend, bold as brass, not a word out of him.

"Two years your mother has given to that residents association. Who was it put a stop to that halting site nonsense. Your mother. Two years out of her life, Ross, and how does she find out that they're planning to shaft her? They're overheard in their plotting. Seems there was a meeting, a clandestine affair it seems, in some coffee shop or other out in Greystones, oh they were all there, Delma, Susan, Hannah, Claudine. Claudine, Ross, can you believe it? Who was it who took her around one of her hot red pepper roulades with ricotta and sundried tomatoes when that King Charles Cavalier of hers died, hmm? Your mother, that's who. Oh, they thought no one would see them, of course, but a friend of your mother's – no names, no pack-drill – let's just say she knows her from bridge, she just happened to be sitting at the table beside them. Overheard everything. Delma, it seems, was the one who actually worded the motion. Susan spent the whole meeting feverishly taking notes in an A4 pad. An A4 pad, if you don't mind."

Oisínn is still holding me back, roysh, while Macker and Fionn are rolling around the floor laughing and suddenly all the goys are coming out of every focking room in the house to find out what's going on. Henno, roysh, this Gonzaga boy, he goes, "I thought it was a focking Denis Leary CD or something". "Like I said, Ross, don't go charging off to the airport or anything. There's nothing you can do. It seems that there are plans afoot to build one of those fearful mobile phone masts at the top of our hill. Could knock about £40,000 off the value of some of our properties. Delma – and we only have the word of our famous eyewitness on this one – she thinks we could have successfully appealed the decision had your mother, as chairperson, been a bit more vigilant.

"Anyway, I took her down to Avoca Handweavers this afternoon. See if I couldn't put a smile back on her face. I mean, you know how much she adores their chicken and tarragon filo bake, Ross. She was like a new woman when we came out of there. Credit card took a bit of a hammering, though. Bought her a beautiful Stephen Pearce earthenware lamp. She had to have it. The clay is dug from the banks of the Blackwater, you know? Passes through eighteen hand-processes along the way. Eighteen, thank you very much indeed. Picked up some of their three-fruit marmalade as well. Delicious. And their walnut, apricot and cinnamon bread, which I was a bit dubious about at first – you remember how dubious I was about it – but it's growing on me. Guess you'd call it an acquired taste.

"And as I mentioned, your mother came home a new woman. I asked her whether she wanted me to have a chat with Hennessy. I mean, he's a lawyer, he'd know straight away whether all these secret meetings and what-not are Constitutional. She said basically no, she's had enough of politics to last her a lifetime. Don't know what she's going to do all day though. I told her I could buy her a shop, like Ted did for Julie, Sorcha's mother. She'd get someone in to manage the thing, of course, but it would keep her occupied. And it's all tax deductible."

The lads will never let me hear the end of this.

Codpiece and the Yeti both ended up having to get second jobs after the, like, bill arrived from the hospital last week. We're talking eight hundred bucks each for the ambulance call-out, we're talking more for treatment in casualty, blah, blah, blah. Codpiece gets onto his old man, roysh, to tell him he's, like, splintered his oesophagus playing rugby or some shit to try to get him to, like, wire over the money? But it turns out, roysh, that his old pair are in Siena for, like, two weeks, we're talking oh my God what a total mare here, and the Yeti didn't want his olds to know, so in the end, roysh, the goys had to go and get jobs at, like, Ocean Pines Golf Club, porking cors and shit?

It's actually not a bad job, roysh, the tips are supposed to be pretty amazing, but the uniforms are a bit skangery. We're talking grey Farah slacks, purple jacket and a black pointed cap. Fionn reckons they look like two gay usherettes heading out for the night.

Anyway, roysh, there we are in the gaff the other day, me and Christian, both on a day off, both totally broke, and I mean totally, sitting in watching *Sally Jesse Raphael*, knocking back a few cans, when all of a sudden this, like, envelope drops through the door and it's, like, a letter from the old man, full of the usual bullshit, roysh. It's like, "Did you manage to see any of the Lions games over there?" and "Hope you're working hard and putting a bit of money aside for college next year" and I was about to burn the focking thing, roysh, when all of a sudden OH MY GOD I notice that there's, like, a cheque in the envelope and I could NOT believe how much it was for, we're talking five hundred focking notes here, and I was, like, so happy I could nearly have sat down there and then and actually finished reading that stupid letter. I said nearly.

The old man is a dickhead and everything, roysh, but the money came bang on time, because we were basically back to living off Cheerios (stale) and Raisin Bran (disgusting) and we're talking breakfast, dinner and tea here, roysh. So me and Christian sat down and talked over how we should, like, spend the money. Should we head down to Foodrite and stock up on provisions or should we go on the complete lash? Should we pay off the electricity bill before they discover that Mad Mal has put, like, a magnet inside the meter or should we go on the complete lash? We went to get changed.

Christian decides we need something a bit strong to get the ball rolling, roysh, so he disappears under the stairs and comes back out with a bottle of Mad Dog 20/20, which he said he was keeping for a special occasion. We knock it back, roysh, do a couple of lines of this new shit that Peasey got from his Detroit connection, hit the bank and then mosey on down to Hooters. The place was fairly packed, I have to say, for four o'clock in the afternoon and we were already pretty buckled by the time we got there. It's actually an amazing bor – we're talking Bap City, Arkansas here – and the waitresses are, like, practically naked and they flirt their orses off with you.

I get chatting to this bird, roysh, this American bird, who I thought looked like Jenny McCarthy, until I got up close and realised she was more like focking Mick McCarthy, but I was actually getting on alright with her, I could tell she was seriously interested in me, and I'm there giving her the old chat-up lines – "the chemistry between us is electric. Can you feel it?" – basically giving it loads until, roysh, she asks me what I'm doing in the States. Obviously I don't want to say I'm actually slaving away for the summer in, like, the steamhouse, roysh, so I tell her I train dolphins and she looks at me really seriously, roysh, and goes, "Oh my God, my ex works in IT too", and I don't even want to know what the fock she's talking about, so when she tells me she's got to go and call her friend Candice I use it as an excuse to fock off and go and look for Christian.

It takes me, like, half an hour to find him, roysh, and when I do he's sitting up at the bor with Sophie and Chloë, who've just come down from Montauk for, like, a holiday in Ocean City and are basically storting to, like, stalk us at this stage and I'm there going to myself, 'What are we doing here? We've both scored the two of them loads of times back home and there's, like, I don't know, a billion other birds in the States who we haven't been with. Let's move on.' But Christian, roysh, who's always had a big thing about Sophie, he's there cracking on to be really interested in what she's saying, which is probably the same old bullshit about home. I slap five bucks and my fake ID on the bor and order a bottle of Bud, then head over to them and Sophie is bitching about some girl who was on the organising committee for the Foxrock predebs with her and used to be sound but has SUCH an attitude problem these days and it's all since she got the jeep.

I stand at the bor beside them and no-one acknowledges me, roysh, not even Christian. Chloë takes a Marlboro Light out of the box and she goes, "Her phone went off once in the middle of German. Me and Ultan were both like, oh my God, TOTAL shamer." Christian asks her who Ultan is and she goes, "He's a really good friend of mine. He's actually gay" and suddenly, roysh, I'm like, "What the fock has that got to do with anything?" And Chloë stops, like, fumbling around in her jacket for her light and she's like, "Sorry, does that make you uncomfortable, Ross, talking about people who are gay?" I'm there, "No, I just don't see what him being gay has to do with the story. It's like if you said, you know, 'He's a really good friend of mine, he's actually got red hair.' I mean, what does it have to do with..." Chloë just goes, "Oh my God, you are SO homophobic, Ross" and she finds her lighter in the pocket of her jacket.

Christian gets a round of drinks in and Sophie asks me whether I've heard from Sorcha and she's basically being a bitch to me. I'm there, "Why would I have heard from Sorcha?" And she goes, "We all got postcards from her. She's having an amazing time. Killian's trying to get her to do the bridge climb" and Chloë goes, "Oh yeah and they went out for dinner in Darling Harbour. She said it was SO romantic." I'm there, "Do I look as though I give a shit?" and the two of them just, like, smile at each other, all delighted with themselves.

I so wanted to fock off at that stage, roysh, but of course four or five pints later, the old beer goggles are on and basically it's obvious that Christian's going to end up being with Sophie and I'm going to end up kissing Chloë, who I think I mentioned earlier actually looks a bit like Heidi Klum. So ten o'clock, roysh, Christian offers the birds a lift home and I pull him aside and I'm like, "HELLO? We can't focking drive in this state. And anyway we don't have a cor." He goes, "Oh yes we do." He tells the chicks we'll be back in a minute, roysh, then we catch a cab up to Ocean Pines Golf Club, bang on time as it happens, because the Yeti is about to pork this big massive eight-litre Viper. This cor, roysh, is an animal and we're talking totally here. I'm there, "We're taking this beast for a little joyride." The Yeti is like, "No FOCKING way, man. There is no FOCKING way you are driving this cor out of here." But I offer him a little persuader, roysh, we're talking a hundred bucks here and he says alright we can go for a spin but only if he's doing the driving.

So the next thing, roysh, we're bombing down Ocean Highway, burning the orse out of the thing, me and the Yeti in the front, Christian and the two birds in the back, heading back to their gaff, pretty much guaranteed our bit, and all of a sudden we hear this siren, roysh, and the cops are behind us telling us to pull over and the Yeti is shitting it because he knows he's going to end up, like, losing his job over this and for about ten seconds, roysh, he actually considers trying to outrun them, but then Sophie says something about Rodney King and at first I think she's asking me to put on a CD, but whoever the fock Rodney King actually is, roysh, the Yeti changes his mind and pulls into the hard shoulder. Sophie goes, "Oh my God, if I get deported my parents are going to go SO ballistic."

Two cops get out. We're totally cacking it. One of them walks up to the driver's window while the other one storts looking the cor over. The cop's like, "Do you know what speed you were doing?" The Yeti's like, "Forty?" He's like, "Are you Irish?" The Yeti goes, "Em, yeah." The cop's there, "So is my grandfawtha, so I know fucking blarney when I hear it, alright? You were going ninety-frickin-five miles an hour. In a forty zone." He goes, "Now, let me see your identification." And Christian, roysh, he leans forward and waves his hand in the cop's face and goes, "You don't need to see his identification." I'm like, 'Fuck, Christian's locked. We're going to end up in focking Sing-Sing.' But all of a sudden, roysh, the cop goes, "We don't need to see his identification." Christian goes, "These aren't the droids you're looking for" and the cop's like, "These aren't the droids we're looking for." And Christian's like, "Move along." The cop goes, "Move along, move along."

Which we did, roysh, and even though we were totally freaked by what had just, like, happened, none of us asked Christian how he'd, like, done it. All he said was, "Thank fock they weren't Tridarians." The Yeti tells us he's bringing the cor back to the golf club right now and he doesn't give a fock how we get back to the gaff and I tell him it's alright, we'll phone a cab from reception and when we go up this big long driveway, roysh, Codpiece is standing in front of the clubhouse, having a total knicker-fit. He's there, "The goy who owns the cor. He came back for it. His wife was in hospital. She'd gone into labour. He kept telling me to fetch his goddam cor fast. I tried to stall him. He knows something's up. He's gone to see the manager. We are SO fired."

The Yeti, roysh, he suddenly goes, "No we're not. We'll tell the boss that the goy's a drug trafficker. And you were just trying to buy some time until the Feds arrived." We all look at the Yeti and I'm like, "What the fock are you talking about?" He pulls out this massive bag of, like, green powder, roysh, which looks suspiciously like the stuff that Peasey had stashed in the water tank in our attic. He opens the dashboard, puts the bag inside it and he goes, "Codpiece, phone 911".

The phones rings, roysh, and I'm actually in the middle of having a shave, but no one else is bothering to answer the thing and I'm basically gicking it in case it's, like, the old man again and I decide I have to get to the phone before it switches to the answer machine. I'm like, "Y'ello?" and I hear the voice on the end of the line and it's, like, Christian's old man and I'm like, "How are you?" He's there, "You don't care how I am. Just put Christian on the line right now." I'm like, "Look, I just wanted to explain." He goes, "I have nothing to say to you. Now go and get my son."

I put the receiver down the table, roysh, and head down to the basement and Christian's lying on his bed with his Walkman on and it's 'Stuck In A Moment', I can hear it, and when he sees me he takes off his headphones and I tell him that his old man's on the phone. I'm, like, totally crapping it, roysh, I'm actually surprised that he can't, like, hear it in my voice. He just goes, "I'm not in" and I'm like, "I think I already told him you were here" and he goes, "Well just tell him I don't want to focking speak to him then." I'm like, "Okay, man. Take a chill pill."

I go back upstairs to the hall, roysh, and I pick up the phone and I'm like, "Em, he says he doesn't want to talk to you." He doesn't answer for ages, roysh, and I go, "You're not going to tell him about..." but suddenly the line goes dead.

MTV's on, roysh, but no-one's really watching it, we're all just spacing, wrecked after the weekend, when all of a sudden Peasey comes in and asks what happened to the bag of green shit that was in the attic. He goes, "You guys sniff that stuff?" looking me and Fionn up and down, as though he's looking for, like, side effects or some shit? I'm like, "We never touched it." I'm looking at Codpiece, roysh, basically telling him to make something up quick, because it was him who took it, but then all of a sudden I notice that the front door's off its hinges – another keg porty last weekend, don't ask – and I'm like, "The place was raided. The Feds."

Peasey throws his hands up, roysh, and he's like, "Hooooly shit." I'm like, "You probably noticed the door on your way in." He doesn't seem to mind about the door, just goes, "You tell em anything?" I'm there, "No." He goes, "You mention my name?" I'm like, "Course I didn't." He goes, "And they took the shit with them?"

Fionn goes, "They didn't charge us or anything. They just said they had to take the stuff away for analysis." He sort of, like, nods, roysh, really slowly, as though he's trying to, like, take this in? Then he goes, "Don't worry, guys. You're safe. Ain't no scientist even heard of that shit yet." On his way out the door, he bumps into Oisínn and he puts on this, like, leprechaun voice and he goes, "Top o'da morning, to ya", even though it's, like, midnight?

Ascelpis Healthcare is this, like, pharmaceutical factory, roysh, where me, Christian and Fionn have just got jobs, we're talking amazing money here, we're talking, like, twenty bills an hour for basically doing fock-all, just letting them use us as sort of guinea pigs to test out all these, like, vaccines they're developing for malaria and shit. Of course if the old man finds out he'll go spare, even though there's, like, fock-all to worry about, although we did all have to sign this, like, waiver, basically saying that if we suddenly grow, I don't know, horns and a focking beak, we've no comeback against the company. But it's only, like, malaria tablets, so we're all there, "Twenty bucks an hour? Where do we sign?"

The thing was, roysh, we SO had to get out of the steamhouse and we're talking totally here. It was REALLY storting to wreck our heads. If I ever see another prawn or mud crab in my life again, I'll just, like, borf my ring up, no bullshitting, so basically we all decided to leave, or rather me, Christian, Fionn, the Yeti and Codpiece decided to leave. Oisínn has only just storted working there and Mad Mal says he doesn't actually mind the smell.

The Yeti and Codpiece got jobs with The Smokers' Alliance, basically hanging out on the boardwalk collecting signatures on this petition supporting smokers' rights. A dollar a signature they got promised by this goy they met at some deck porty at Fagors Island. They ended up getting a LOAD of names. We're talking three and a half thousand here. The thing is, roysh, Codpiece is a bit of a charmer when it comes to the opposite sex and he'd have got a load just from, like, using some of his old chat-up lines, and you'd never say no to the Yeti if you saw this goy coming towards you, big seven foot focker, you'd basically shit yourself. Codpiece says he grabbed some goy who refused to sign the petition by the scruff of the neck, slammed him up against a lamppost, gave him the pen and, like, made him sign, even guiding the goy's hand on the page, the mad bastard.

So they ended up doing that and me and the goys ended up going for this job that we saw in the *Ocean City Advertiser*. It was like,

*BROKE? OUT OF WORK? RENT DUE?*
*ASCELPIS HEALTHCARE IS CURRENTLY*
*RECRUITING YOUNG PEOPLE*
*WITH A VIEW TO CONDUCTING*
*MEDICAL EXPERIMENTS ON THEM.*
*WHY NOT GIVE US A CALL?*
*YOU'VE NOTHING TO LOSE* \*

And underneath, in small writing, roysh, it was like:

*   some weight reduction and hair loss may occur, though both conditions are thought to be temporary*

So we phoned the freephone number and the next thing, roysh, the three
of us are sitting in this goy's office, we're talking the head of research in the
company, roysh, and the first thing he asks us is like, "Do you guys drink?"
We all look at each other, delighted, roysh, and Christian goes, "Yeah, alright,
I'll have a Heineken." And the goy, something McPhee his name was, big fat
bastard with a red face, he looks a bit embarrassed, roysh, and he's like, "Em,
I'm just taking your personal details. I'm not asking whether you want...
Look, I'll level with you guys and you can decide right now whether we're
wasting one another's time. One of the requirements of the medical research
programme is that you abstain from alcohol."

I'm about to get up and leave, roysh, basically too honest for my own
good, but all of a sudden Fionn goes, "Actually, none of us drink, which makes
me believe that we're ideal candidates for the job." He says this with a straight
face and then he pushes his glasses up on his nose. The goy looks at the three
of us, roysh, we were out on the lash last night and I'm sure he can focking
smell the drink of us, but he just goes, "Alriiiight", as though he can't make up
his mind whether to hire us or call security, but then all of a sudden he's just
like, "Okay, boys. Welcome to the firm. Come on, I'll show you where you'll be
working."

So there we are, roysh, wandering down all these corridors and he's
telling us all this shite about how long the company has been established,
blah blah blah, and Christian turns around and goes, "Tell us a bit about
these malaria pills you're making," and the goy suddenly stops walking and
goes, "Excuse me?" Christian's like, "The malaria pills" and the goy goes,
"What malaria pills?" Christian goes, "I just thought..." And the bloke's like,
"We don't talk about products that haven't been passed by the FDA. Ground
rule number one. It's best that you know nothing about these pills. In fact, it'd
be better all round if you forgot my name. And what I look like."

Christian all of a sudden stops, roysh, and he's like, "Goys, I have a
baaaad feeling about this." Me and Fionn are there, "Christian, we need the
focking money." He's like, "There must be another way." This goy McPhee,
roysh, he goes, "Is there a problem?" and I'm like, "Just give us a minute with

him and we'll be okay" and he sort of, like, makes himself scarce, roysh, and I turn to Christian and I'm like, "What did you have for dinner yesterday?" He goes, "You know what I had for dinner yesterday." I'm there, "Just FOCKING tell me. What did you have?" He's like, "A bowl of Cinnamon Grahams. Same as the night before." I'm like, "And the night before that. Well tonight, Christian, you're having a change. There's no milk left. So it's Cinnamon Grahams with water. That's until the Cinnamon Grahams run out. And then..."

He goes, "Look, all I'm saying is there must be other ways of earning money." Fionn goes, "There aren't, Christian. Look, we'll get this fat focker to sub us a hundred bucks each out of our wages. Think what that'll mean. A hot meal tonight. Think about it. We won't have to hide under the stairs when Peasey comes around for the rent. We'll be able to take the magnet off the electricity meter. Come on, Christian, what do you say?" He thinks for a minute, roysh, and then he goes, "Okay. But if I stort growing hairs on the palms of my focking..." Fionn's like, "Christian, you worry too much."

The boss man comes back. He's like, "All sorted out, boys?" and we're like, "Yeah", and he brings us into this room, roysh, this sort of, like, play-room, with this big fock-off television and video, computer games, the whole lot. I'm like, "This is where we're going to be, like, working?" He goes, "Yep. There's nothing to the job, I told you that. You take a couple of pills in the morning. We hook you up to a heart monitor and you spend the rest of the day in here, watching the television, playing Nintendo, whatever you want. End of the day, we take a blood and urine test from you and then you go home. Look, I'll leave you guys to get acquainted with the place."

He focks off, roysh, and me, Christian and Fionn just look at each other and break our shites laughing. Fionn pushes his glasses up on his nose and he's like, "A hundred and sixty bucks a day. To watch *Jenny Jones* and *The Love Boat* and play video games..." I'm like, "We've struck gold, goys." And about half-an-hour later, roysh, the boss comes back into the room and he goes, "I've got your waivers here to sign. And by the way, I didn't mention it before but we pay extra money for sperm and stool samples." Christian goes, "And we shall provide. We SHALL provide."

Me, Chrisian, Oisínn and Fionn, we were in, like, Starbucks last week-end, roysh, and I clearly heard Oisínn ask for a caffé Americano, which is basically just espresso with, like, hot water in it, but the goy serving us, roysh, who obviously doesn't speak a word of focking English, he brings him out a chocolate brownie frappuccino and me Christian, we just stort giving Oisínn loads, basically calling him a faggot and shit. So Fionn calls the goy over, roysh, and tells him he got the order wrong, but the goy's there going, "This what you ask for. This what you ask for", and he refuses to change it, even though we all CLEARLY heard him say caffé Americano.

So Oisínn, roysh, he goes, "I want to speak to the manager. Not the minimum wage lackey", which he actually had a bit of a cheek saying, roysh, considering he's the only one of us still peeling prawns for, like, shit money. The goy goes, "I am manager. So drink your coffee or you go out." Oisínn, roysh, who doesn't put up with shit from anyone, he gets his elbow and, like, knocks the coffee onto the floor, sort of like accidentally on purpose and he goes, "Hey, skivvy. Get your mop and bucket. Looks like you're about to earn another gold star."

And the goy, roysh, he goes ballistic and we are talking totally here. He hops over the counter, grabs Oisínn and tries to, like, hustle him out of the shop and me, Fionn and Christian are like, 'That is SO not on. Nobody treats Castlerock boys like that", even though he hordly needed our help, being the big focker that he is. But we follow them outside anyway, roysh, and I'm about to suggest we phone my old man to get, like, his solicitor on the case, when all of a sudden Oisínn slams the goy up against the wall and Fionn all of a sudden focks a brick through the window of the place.

Oh my God all hell breaks loose then. You will not believe what happened. Basically we hadn't noticed, roysh, but there was some kind of focking protest march going through the town at that exact time, anti-globalisation or some shit, so there was all these, like, students and shit gagging for a riot, roysh, and they thought Fionn breaking the window was, like, us kicking the whole thing off, so the next thing all these bricks and petrol bombs are flying about the place and I'm, like, caught up in the whole thing, the old animal instincts taking over, and I'm basically running amok in The Gap, robbing sweatshirts, jeans, the whole lot, while Fionn and Christian set up, like, a barricade on the road outside.

Of course, someone calls the cops, roysh, and they arrive and catch me looting the focking place and it's like, "Drop those baseball caps and hit the floor, you mother" and I get down on the ground, roysh, which is basically when I see the damage for the first time. The place is like a focking bomb zone, glass and all sorts of shit all over the gaff. So we're brought off to the cop shop, roysh, MUCH nicer than Donnybrook it has to be said, though memories of the Freshers' Ball came flooding back when the cop put me in the cell and told me to, like, cool off. So I'm sitting there for, like, four or five hours, roysh, when they come and tell me that I'm entitled to a phone call and I decide to ring the old man, roysh, just to break the news about him having to go bail for me. He goes focking ballistic of course. I tell him I was arrested for, like, jaywalking, roysh, but the cop who put through the call must have already told him the real reason because he goes, "I can't believe it, Ross. I can't believe it." I'm like, "It's only a focking window, dad. Five or six hundred squids, that's all it's going to cost you. Get over it, will you?"

He's, like, bawling his eyes out, though, the complete dickhead, and he's going, "Oh forget about the window, Ross, that can be fixed. Unlike other things. You were involved in, I can hardly even bring myself to say it, an ANTI-CAPITALIST demonstration." I tell him it was more of an anti-chocolate-brownie-frappuccino demonstration but he doesn't get the joke, the knob that he is. He goes, "Capitalism is the foundation stone of our democracy, Ross. Capitalism is freedom of speech and thought. Freedom to make money and not be bloody well ashamed of it. It's what separates us from the likes of Kerrigan and his mob. Oh, I knew I shouldn't have kept bringing that paper into the house. It was your mother, you see. She loves that Patricia Redlich and..." I just hang up on the dickhead, I mean fock bail, twenty years in jail would have been better than twenty more seconds of that.

So anyway, roysh, I'm back in my cell, basically sitting there, pretty much resigned to the fact that I'm going to be, like, sewing focking mailsacks for the rest of the summer, when all of a sudden this cop comes in and tells me they're letting us all go. It turns out that Christian, the complete focking spacer, had confessed under questioning to intercepting transmissions that exposed a fatal flaw in the defences of the Death Star and the cops basically decided that we weren't the masterminds behind the anti-globalisation demonstrations after all. I mean, it would hordly have taken the FBI to figure that out after, like, five minutes in a room with Christian, who actually used his phonecall to ring one of those premium rate numbers giving out information on the new *Star Wars* movie.

To cut a long story short, roysh, we're out in the sort of, like, reception area, getting our stuff back and one of the cops, who's, like, the sheriff or something, he's apologising to Fionn on behalf of the people of Ocean City and when we get outside, roysh, I ask him why the cops were being so nice and why there was nothing about us having to pay for the window and shit? It turns out, roysh, that Fionn had the old school bible with him, this book they give you when you leave Castlerock and it has, like, the names and numbers of past pupils living all over the world who you can, like, ring if you're ever in trouble.

Fionn used his phonecall to ring this goy, Tristan Dardis, who's, like, some big knob in the mayor's office. "The second I rang him," he goes, pushing his glasses up on his nose, "there was a complete change in the attitude of the cops towards us." Oisínn all of a sudden starts breaking his shite laughing, roysh, and I ask him what's so funny and he goes, "They asked me did I want coffee. You won't believe this, but they even asked me how I liked it."

I get home from work and there's, like, post for me and it's, like, a letter from the old man, which I sort of, like, scan through really quickly – please try to stay out of trouble, bullshit bullshit bullshit – and then I drop it in the bin, roysh, but there's also a postcord in the envelope and it's from Sorcha. I stare at the front of it for ages, roysh. It's, like, the Opera House, I think, and loads of other, like, skyscrapers and shit and on the front it says, "City skyline from Kirribilli, Sydney" and I head into my room and lie on the bed and read the back ten, maybe twenty times.

Sorcha says she's having the time of her life, even though it's pretty cold over there because it's, like, winter and shit? She's working in, like, Golden Pages, roysh, or whatever the equivalent of it is over there, basically taking ads over the phone. She's only going to be able to work there for, like, three months, roysh, unless they offer to sponsor her, which they probably won't and she doesn't care because she SO wants to travel and basically see a bit of Australia, especially Cairns and the Gold Coast, which she says are supposed to be amazing.

She says she might be doing the bridge climb next weekend, even though she's, like, really scared of heights and she says she wouldn't mind getting four or five bottles of Smirnoff Ice into her first, but they actually breathalyse you before they let you do it, and she says that Dorling Harbour is amazing, especially at night, but she was really disappointed with Bondi Beach, which is basically a dump and a bit of an Irish ghetto and that's the reason she's pretty much staying away from it. And I notice, roysh, that she hasn't mentioned that Killian dickhead once and at the end, roysh, she says she really misses me and after her name she's put, like, three kisses.

I hear the rest of the goys coming in from work, roysh, so I slip the cord into my back pocket and tell Fionn and Oisínn that I'm heading down to Foodrite because we need, like, beers and I head down to Candy's, this diner down the road from our gaff, and I order coffee and sit there, in one of the, like, cubicles, reading the cord over and over again, then taking it line by line, trying to pick up, like, hidden meanings that may or may not have been there, then just studying her handwriting, the real neat sort of, like, convent school strokes, trying to imagine what was going through her head when she said that she missed me, whether she put that on everyone's cord or whether she really meant it in my case, and what she was thinking when she put those, like, three kisses on it?

I stort to think about going home, which I'm dreading, for loads of different reasons, but one in particular, and I think about maybe never going home, staying on in Ocean City for a few months and saving up enough money to go to Australia myself and see how serious things are between Sorcha and this asshole she's seeing. I take off my baseball cap and scratch my head and a huge clump of hair comes off in my hand and I just, like, drop it onto the floor under the table and read the cord again, and suddenly I hear Candy going, "Stare at that any lawnga and the print's gonna come awf. You want more cawfee?"

I'm in the jacks in work, roysh, basically sitting in one of the cubicles having a shit, when all of a sudden the door opens and someone comes in and then I hear Christian going, "What are you doing, Ross, ones or twos?" He goes into trap two and I hear him, like, undoing his belt and his trousers and sitting down. I'm like, "Em, twos." He goes, "Panning for gold, huh?" I'm there, "Sure." I can hear him opening a newspaper. After a couple of minutes of rustling, he goes, "Hey, Ross. When he said they pay for stool samples, do they pay for each one or is it based on, like, tonnage?" I'm like, "He didn't specify." He goes, "You'd think he would have, wouldn't you? Could save an embarrassing court case some way down the line." I'm like, "Sure."

Christian goes back to reading his paper and I go back to reading the graffiti on the wall. There must have been, like, loads of Irish students working here before us, because there's a couple of names I recognise and the rest is, like, bands, the usual, Smashing Pumpkins, U2, Eminem, all that stuff, and then a couple of old jokes that I've seen loads of times before, like "Dyslexia rules KO."

I hear someone else come in and he tries Christian's door and then mine, just to make sure there's someone in there, then whoever it is just goes to the sink and washes his hands and probably checks himself out in the mirror but doesn't, like, use the hand dryer, which means he probably just, like, wiped his hands on his trousers or in his hair. When the goys leaves, roysh, Christian completely out of the blue goes, "I'm thinking of ringing my old man." This sudden, like, nausea hits me. I'm not sure if it's what he just said or whether it's, like, the tablets and shit? I'm there, "You've forgiven him then?" He goes, "Maybe I've been a bit hard on him. I mean, he obviously had his reasons for going." I'm there, "Yeah but it's going to be very difficult for you to sort it out over the phone. Maybe you should just wait till you go home. It's only another three weeks."

He goes, "I suppose that makes sense." I stand up and look into the toilet, roysh, and my shit is, like, yellow. Christian goes, "How much, Ross?" I just, like, flush it away. I'm there, "Couldn't go. Looks like I'm staying in tonight."

You-know-who left another message on the answering machine, roysh, and basically my blood ran cold when I heard it, hairs standing up on the back of my neck, goosebumps, the whole lot. It's like, "Ross, em, your mother wanted me to, em, ask you, it's delicate, a bit embarrassing, but there's a certain rumour going around about, well, Christian's mother and father, or Christian's mother mostly. Alice. Oh it's nothing of course, just rumours as I said, I'm sure there's nothing in it, it's just that people are saying that the reason they broke up, or one of the reasons they broke up – it's never really one thing that breaks up a marriage – the reason was that... well look, maybe you should just ring your mother. Have a chat with her. She listens to people, you see, and she shouldn't. And she's upset anyway about the car. Failed the NCT. If it's not one thing it's another.

"She was disconsolate, Ross. With a capital d. I told her I'd buy her a new one, but no. If she couldn't have her Micra, she didn't want anything. Took to the bed for three days. Now I'm not what you would call inverted-commas anti the environment, Ross, you know that. But this whole car test business is nothing more than a money-making scam by the government, basically to force people to buy new cars. Dress it up as an environmental concern, fuel emissions and so forth, and nobody dares to complain. I phoned up the so-called Department of the Environment on Monday morning. Asked to speak to the minister but ended up getting some bloody minion. As if the Government doesn't get enough money out of me already, I said I employ over 200 people. It's the law, he said. BUT YOU MADE THE BLOODY LAW, I told him. Hung up on me, he did.

"To be honest, Ross, don't breathe a word of this to anyone, but I pretty much knew the car was going to fail. I mean, I myself personally was against the idea of buying her a second hand car in the first place, but she said she only wanted a little runaround and once she saw the Micra, well, she would-n't have anything else. But oh the day of the test was painful, Ross. Like a funeral it was. And it was in bloody Deansgrange as well, appropriately enough. An 8.30am appointment, quote-unquote. I won't bore you with the details, Ross, but we drove into the industrial estate, parked the car outside and this chap in green overalls came out and asked your mother for the keys. Of course getting them out of her hand was a job in itself, but eventually, using a few stern words, not to mention the car-jack, we managed to loosen her grip on them and then the chap drove the car into this garage affair and I helped your mother into the office, where they asked for our details and the logbook. 'When will you know?' your mother asked the lady behind the desk. Forty-five minutes, the lady said. It was an hour at least and your mother spent the whole time pacing up and down the floor, asking me every five min-utes what I thought was keeping them. 'They have a lot of checks to make, I told her. 'Sit down. Read a magazine. Look, *VIP* have done an 18-page feature on 'At Home with IFA farm leader Tom Parlon.'

"Well, the bad news was that the chap returned after what seemed like an eternity, all full of himself with his clipboard, and delivered the verdict. Wheel alignment, front axle – FAIL. Wheel alignment, rear axle – FAIL. Shock absorber, front axle – FAIL. Shock absorber, rear axle – FAIL. Brake test, front and rear axle – FAIL. Service brake performance — 40% and FAIL. Parking brake performance – 10% and FAIL. Exhaust emissions – FAIL. Right indicator, steering lock, tyre pressure, windscreen wipers – all defective, FAIL. Dip beam, full beam, fog lights – FAIL, FAIL, FAIL.

"It was too much for your mother, of course. She collapsed. And while the staff tried to resuscitate her, I got on the phone, called the bloody gangster we bought the car from in the first place. 'Good morning', he says, without a care in the world. 'I haven't got time for good-mornings,' I told him. 'I think you know why I'm phoning.' 'Em, I don't', he said, just out with it like that. I told him I'd a complaint to make about a car he sold me. 'What's the matter with it?' he said. What's the matter with it, ladies and gentlemen. 'Pretty much everything except the radio, according to the NCT people. And even that chewed one of my Phil Coulter cassettes a couple of months ago.' 'When did you buy the car?' he asked. '1993?' I told him. 'Sorry,' he says, 'did you say 1993?' 'That is what I said, yes. 'Well, seven years is a long time to get out of a second hand car,' he said. 'And the warranty doesn't...' That was it. 'I don't care about your blasted warranty,' I said. 'You told me the car had one previous owner. An elderly lady who used it to get to the shops and back.' 'Yeah,' he says. 'Where were the bloody shops?" I asked him. 'Kosovo?'

"I offered the car test chap a couple of hundred pounds to, well, basically pass the car, but he got all offended and told me that kind of thing was illegal, bloody tribunal culture has a lot to answer for, thank you very much indeed. But well, I think that's what has your mother so upset, not this business about Christian's mother... You know the way people like to gossip. Especially at those coffee mornings of hers... I told her it was all... But you should call her, Ross. Even just to put her mind at rest."

What happened between me and Christian's mum wasn't actually my fault. Okay, I didn't exactly fight her off, roysh, but basically she was the one who made a move on me and I'm the one who, like, ends up the villain. Christian's old man is basically an asshole, roysh, who's been doing the dirt on her for years, not just with that woman he worked with, the partner in the company he works in, there was also this other bird he played tennis with in Riverview and then this other one who was, like, Christian's mum's best friend since they were, like, ten or something. It doesn't excuse what happened, roysh, but Christian's old man is basically a focking hypocrite if he tells Christian about it.

It happened at, like, Iseult's twenty-first, roysh, we're talking Iseult as in Christian's sister here, about three years ago. The porty was in their gaff,

roysh, on Ailesbury Road and it was obvious that the old pair had had a massive row earlier in the day, you could tell that from the atmosphere in the gaff
and the way the two of them were drinking. Basically I don't know what
Christian's old man said to her, roysh, but I went to use the downstairs jacks
and there was someone in there, so I headed for the other one upstairs and
when I pushed the door there was something blocking it, a pair of legs, basically Christian's mother sitting on the side of the bath bawling her eyes out.

I went in, roysh, and she was, like, totally locked and she storts, like,
pouring her whole life out to me, about what Christian's old man was really
like, about that woman who had the cheek to come into her house on this of
all days and, like, I wasn't sure who she was talking about, though it must
have been someone that the old man was basically knocking off on the side?

I sat on the bath beside her, roysh, and the next thing we were, like, kissing each other and, you know, I'll spare you the details but basically one thing
led to another. It was weird, roysh, because I never actually fancied her, not
really, she wasn't a yummy-mummy like Simon's old dear, not being a bastard or anything but she actually looked her age, which was, like, mid-forties,
expensive jewellery, make-up packed on. But anyway, roysh, it happened
there in the bathroom, the two of us there doing it and me gicking it in case
Christian or his old man or, fock, his granny even, came up to use the toilet.
When it was over she said it was lovely, she goes, "That was lovely", but I
knew it was bullshit, it was over too quick for it to have been lovely.

And that was it, we both headed back downstairs to the porty and it was
never mentioned again, roysh, and even when I was in the gaff after that there
was no, like, awkwardness about it, and sometimes I wondered whether she
was too pissed to even remember, because it was just like it never happened
and shit? That was until the day before we came away, roysh, when she basically phoned me up at home and said she'd told Christian's old man what
happened. She said she was sorry. It was all bound to come out now, she said.
Christian would find out, because his old man would use it to worm his way
back into Christian's good books. They'd had a blazing row on the phone
apparently, when she found out that he never actually finished with the bird
he was seeing from work that time, it had gone on for years, two of her friends
from tennis told her, and in the heat of the argument she told him what happened at Iseult's porty three years ago.

And now I don't want to go home. I want to stay here or maybe go to Australia but I ruined things with Sorcha just as I've ruined them with Christian,

the two people in my life I love the most, and I've been, like, so depressed late-ly, my moods are really, like, dark and shit, and maybe that has something to do with the tablets, or maybe it's a mixture of the tablets, the drink and the Max-Alerts, but some days I just want to phone up everyone I've ever met in my life and tell them I'm sorry, and then other days I want to just, like, smash up our gaff and....

And me and Christian are sitting there watching *Jenny Jones*, roysh, and there's this bloke on it who's telling his bird that he's been, like, sleeping with her sister for years, roysh, and I know that me and Christian's friendship is coming to an end, which is one of the reasons why I just want time to stand still, so we never have to go home, him to face his parents' divorce and me to face, well, basically the music, and I focking hate myself for not having the guts to tell him what I've done.

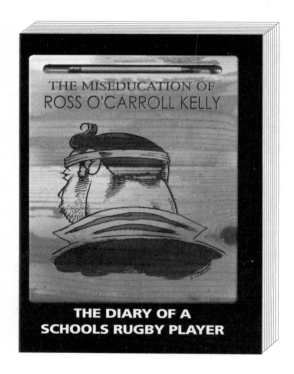